Wake Up and Smell the Competition ... They're Closer Than You Think!

by

Christine Corelli

Cardinal Business Press

Wake Up and Smell the Competition ...
They're Closer Than You Think
By Christine Corelli

Copyright ©2000 Christine Corelli & Associates, Inc.
First U. S. Edition published September 2000

ISBN: 0-9700080-0-7

Published by
Cardinal Business Press
Chicago, IL
(800) 611-9968
(See page 196 for ordering information)

Printed in the United States of America

Table of Contents

Dedication

This book is dedicated to my son, Jeffrey Joseph Barloga. His mere existence has kept me on a "straight and narrow" path and made me want to become an Achiever. Thank you for giving me the gift of desire to excel.

Acknowledgements

This book would not have been possible without the encouragement and support of a number of special people. First, my thanks to David Shepherd for creatively editing and making it a reality. To Bruce Olson, Barry Eigen, Tony Stubbs and Robert Darling—their help in editing and providing feedback contributed much to its content. I am also indebted to Melissa Giovagnali, not only for her contribution to this book, but also for guiding me into my career. To my loyal friend Barbara Friedman, who not only supported me with this endeavor but also gave me twenty years of true friendship, and never once failed to catch me before I'd fall.

My gratitude to my other dear colleagues and friends whose help and cheerleading regarding this book were unfaltering: Larry Salani, Pat Salani, Bob Gnal, Norell Cefalu, and Bob Hovan. Also thanks to Laurie Guest, Robert Shapiro, Jeffrey Gitomer, Doug Dvorak, Barbara Glanz, Mike Wynne, Mark LeBlanc, C. Leslie Charles, Allen Sells, Richard Thieme, and Cyndi Maxey.

To my valued clients with whom I discussed my ideas and who generously shared their experiences and beliefs—I thank you.

To all my teachers, mentors, beloved friends and family who believed in me— often before I believed in myself: Jeffrey, Jessica and Natalie Barloga, Richard Shepherd, Keith McCawle, Carol Conti, the Kordowski's and the Webers, Dr. John Powers, Dotti Hovan, Jim Meisenheimer, Frank Bucaro, Donna Hovan, Carl Huffman, Edward Madden, Carol Greiter, Frank and Fran Turco, Gayle Olson, (Gayle, - Queenie, you are gone but never forgotten. I miss you every day of my life. There will never be another you!)

Also, Charlene Gorzela, Lea Minalga, Margo Pachona, Wendy Vanderbilt, Anna Turco, Sam Geist, Robert and Terri Cefalu, Marion and Ken Keller, Marie Cozzi, Laura Farina, Ian, Kyle, Allison, Alex, Christopher, and Carlos and Debbie Contreras.

Last, but not least, to my parents, Joseph and Antoinette Minnala, who instilled in me a strong sense of right and wrong.

To all these people I owe a debt of gratitude for all their support and encouragement. I hope I have given you much in return. Each of you holds a special place in my heart that I carry wherever I go.

Foreword

I have been privileged to know Ms. Christine Corelli for many years. She is an incredibly talented speaker and author as well as a highly valued consultant to numerous organizations. No matter how many times I witness one of her presentations, I am always awed by her knowledge, insights and a speaking style that never fails to open the minds or warm the hearts of every member of her audience.

Christine speaks from experience and a perspective of common sense that is so often lacking in today's business world. Like all artists, she is one-of-a-kind and, once personally experienced, never to be forgotten. Her outlooks are the answers to many of the problems that plague businesses and business people today.

Christine has transformed her insights, experience, common sense observations and expertise into this wonderful reading adventure. After you take the adventure, you will want to read it again, tell others about it and no, you will not be willing to lend them your copy.

— Dr. John R. Powers, playwright, novelist,
and professional speaker

Preface

So you've picked up this book and now you're wondering if it's for you. Are you interested in maximizing your potential for success and learning how to help position yourself and your company head and shoulders above your competitors? If you need a push into reality and a shove away from complacency, are overwhelmed by the pace of our fast-changing business world and would like to make an impact in your organization, then this is definitely the book for you. It can be read over a weekend and give you business savvy for a lifetime. That sounds like a pretty good return on investment to me. This book will give you and your company a boost—like a great cup of Starbucks coffee in the morning.

On my journey from being a shy, introverted young girl from a working class family to a successful performing artist, trade show sales specialist, entrepreneur and international business speaker, I've made my share of mistakes, but I've also learned a lot from this diverse background. My purpose in writing this book is to share some of the business experience I have acquired that I believe will help you to compete and win in today's tough business world—just as I have. Many of these ideas are responsible for my own success. As you read, think of others who may benefit from its message, as my diverse business clients have repeatedly told me it contains relevant content both they and their people need. I hope you will find value in reading it.

— Christine Corelli

Introduction

Let's take a good hard look at the reality of today. We're living and working in a world where mergers, acquisitions, and downsizing have become the norm. The Internet and the World Wide Web have leveled the playing field for most companies, and tilted the scales for others. Apart from facilitating the free transmission of information and changing us into a "networked" society, consider what it's done to the selling and distribution of our products and services. It has allowed smaller businesses to flourish and compete with larger companies. Just as small speedboats can run circles around huge oil tankers, today's small businesses can now compete against large companies. One reason for this is that a visitor to a company's web site has no idea of the size of the company. Also, small companies are unencumbered by bureaucratic decision-making. And new corporations pop up every day consisting of just one person sitting behind a computer.

The global marketplace is sleepless, selling and competing around the clock, seven days a week. New markets and customer bases are being created overnight. For these reasons, the challenge for companies today lies in the difficulty of long-range planning. Conditions change so quickly that predicting outcomes is difficult.

Today, the Internet allows us to know what our competitors are up to, and vice versa. Back in my trade-show days, I recall sales managers giving phony badges to their technical people and telling them to sneak around their competitors' booths and attempt to fool an unsuspecting soul into giving them their literature. Today, you don't need to be a 007 to learn about your competitors—you just need a modem.

Easy communication through the Internet makes geographic location much less important and has eliminated the need for the middleman. With a computer, a carpet-weaver in the Andes can now sell directly to a store in New York. Depending on the industry, the Internet has also eliminated much of the need for field sales calls, unless there's a new product involved or a problem has arisen.

No matter what industry we're in, we all work harder for our money, but today's sales professionals are a whole new breed. Selling is getting more competitive every minute due to more suppliers offering more choices, more ways to purchase, higher customer expectations and increased price resistance to overcome. We must do much more than sell—we must add *value* by providing service, helping with product selection, and even offering to package our products. Solving customers' problems is also key.

Most important, today's sales pros must not only develop strong customer relationships that will enhance customer loyalty, but they must also help their companies find cutting-edge solutions to any product or service problems that may exist. They must arm themselves with industry knowledge and know their competitors intimately. If they want to earn their commission, all of this is required of today's top sales professionals.

The Internet has affected every business, every industry, and every person. For example, in an effort to ward off competition from vendors who have begun to offer their products on their own web sites, some large discount retailers are warning these suppliers that they may retaliate by looking for alternative sources.

The number of consumers now ordering products over the Internet is astounding. Look at the incredible success of companies like Dell and Gateway. First, consumers have been fast to realize that they can often avoid sales tax and that ordering through the Internet is easier than going to a large discount retailer, where they must not only find a parking space but also try to find a salesperson with enough product knowledge to fully answer their questions. (Recently, I purchased a new computer from a well-known retail establishment. The salesman encouraged me to spend an extra twenty-five dollars for the upgrade version of their operating system. He didn't even know it came already installed.) Purchasers must then stand in line to pay, something that often takes longer than selecting the product.

Most of the current mass-market retail models leave consumers confused, dissatisfied and hungry for information. The Internet provides them with answers to questions and 24-hour shopping convenience at competitive prices. However, innovative mass-market retailers, such as Circuit City, allow customers to place their order on the Internet then pick it up at their store without the hassle. Office Depot delivers Internet orders within 24 hours.

Of course, many consumers will always want to shop at a well-merchandised store where they can touch and feel the products, but many others are "click-happy" online shopaholics who order everything from champagne to snowboards. And, let's not forget about the Customer of the Future, the younger generation who will do most of their shopping the same way they do everything else—on the Internet.

Advances in telecommunications, computer hardware, and other sophisticated technologies have brought us into an *Era of Speed.* These technologies are supposed to make us more efficient while relieving us from mundane tasks. However, the speed and ubiquity of these devices have not fully lived up to their promise. We were meant to be a paperless society, but paper consumption is increasing, and paperwork clutters our desks to the point of distraction. Because we are now choreographed to move, work, learn, receive information and service our customers instantly, it's tougher than ever for everyone.

Because today's consumers have access to information via the Internet, they're better informed, more discriminating, and more demanding than ever. They know that if they can't get what they want, how they want it, when they want it, and at the price they're willing to pay for it, then the Web will show them where to go. The impact of technology has been phenomenal! Who knows where it will lead us as ever more sophisticated technologies emerge? Every issue of *Futurist* magazine contains articles that describe some of the new incredible technologies that will emerge in the not too distant future.

Our workforce has also changed. In this *Era of Continuous Improvement,* the majority of businesses are in a desperate race for growth, and people feel the pressure to perform. No longer do loyalty and hard work automatically translate into job security. In a tight job market, technical workers evolve as the elite of the workforce. Blue-collar jobs are being made redundant by robotics, flexible machine tools, and automated inventory management systems while others are outsourced to low-wage countries.

The trend-forecasters tell us that the blue-collar or *Industrial Revolution* took 120 years. And that the white-collar revolution, now well underway, will take ten to fifteen years, and when it's over, 90 percent of all white-collar jobs either will be radically different or won't even exist. The new paradigm of the workplace is that it will never be the same—it will be reinvented daily as global technology and opportunity unfold.

In this environment where competition is fierce and businesses are in a race for growth with no finish line in sight, organizations and individuals are asking some hard questions, such as:

- What attitudes and mind-sets will serve us best?

- What knowledge and skills will we need to outperform the competition?

- How can we prevent losing ground to those fast companies in hot pursuit?

- How can we obtain life-balance and enjoy personal success?

- How will we be able to compete and WIN?

The remainder of this book answers these questions. Now I fully realize that each chapter could have been extended into an entire book but my purpose is to share what's worked for me and my clients that will most benefit you, the reader. It's not intended to impress business people with complex theories and technical jargon. We've all read too many books where writers become absorbed in esoteric discussions punctuated by confusing flowcharts. Rather, it's a simple-to-read, easy-to-understand discussion of what I have observed and teach in my seminars.

Section 1

Tune Up Your
Mind to Win

6:00 a.m.: The alarm goes off and you wake up feeling as if you just got into bed. How could this be? You slept eight hours, yet you're still fatigued and too weary to even think of going to the gym before work today.

7:00 a.m.: You're stuck in traffic. In the last twenty minutes, you've moved only twenty feet.

8:00 a.m.: You walk into the office and are greeted by disgruntled people who are still complaining about last month's budget cuts. You pour yourself a cup of coffee and proceed to your dreary gray "cube" (some call it a cell) and immediately become stressed out looking at yesterday's unfinished work and the nagging voice-mail light flashing on your phone.

You open your e-mail and see some 30 messages, mostly from people requesting an immediate response, and your finger is begging simply to hit the delete key. The delete key does zap the e-mail from well-meaning friends with those humorous or motivational messages. Even though you could use a laugh or a boost for your morale, you simply don't have the time to read them.

You have an important customer meeting at 9:00 a.m. and you haven't finished your preparation. Buried under mounds of paperwork and to-dos, is a memo from your sales manager to inform you that you've lost a valuable account to your toughest competitor. He's asking what went wrong. Although you desperately need an assistant to type an important proposal, you simply don't have one and must frantically whip it out yourself before your meeting. You wonder why the company sent you to that time management seminar that stressed the importance of effective delegation. To whom would you delegate—the invisible man?

9:00 a.m.: You walk into the meeting with a phony smile on your face and a knot in your stomach. The only thing you can think about is that it's only 9:00 a.m. and you realize that, with all the work you have to do, you'll be working late again.

Sounds all too familiar, right? Well, don't feel bad. The sad truth is that it's the norm for all too many people these days. In today's fast-paced, highly competitive marketplace, we're expected to do more things in less time and with fewer resources than ever before. When was the last time your boss said, "Listen, I know you said you can increase sales by 10% next month, but I don't think you should work so hard. Tell you what, just give me a 3% increase over the next four months, and that will be good enough." Probably not recently, huh?

Perhaps you're a new manager who's been told, "Here's your desk, here's your phone, here's your computer, here's your people! Make sure they're highly motivated and productive, even though we know most are doing the job two people should be doing. Make sure they know how to work together as a team because there's a lot of dissension and animosity here. They received little direction and appreciation from the last manager. Even though there's a lot of nit-picking going on, make sure they're polite to customers. And, be sure it's understood we expect you to put in sixty hours a week like the rest of management. Oh, and by the way, the monthly figures will never be good enough, and the budget and forecasts are merely a wish-list made up of wild guesses."

Or maybe you're a small business owner who is financed to the hilt, and lie awake at night worrying how you can stay afloat. Everywhere you turn, new competitors are opening their doors. You think about how your employees have been productive and loyal. And just like you, they have spouses, kids in college, and mortgages to pay. You pray you can increase your business without going under in the process.

Imagine you are my client who experienced this: You're a branch manager for a manufacturing organization whose profits are down, but your branch is one of the two keeping the company going. Some genius came up with the idea that they should cut some jobs in design, supervision, and service. You knew this would be a short-term fix for the problem, even though the company felt that the cuts would result in quick returns. You knew the people who proposed the cuts and made the decisions would not necessarily be held accountable for the actual outcome. Could they possibly assume sales would stay the same, that customers would remain loyal, and that new product development could be put on hold for a few months? Could they not see the error in their thinking? Did they think their product is so clever that only they could make it? Did they not consider that the customer may not be willing to wait for the time it would take to produce it? Did they think customers would pay whatever price they asked or consider what this might do to employee morale?

You decided to put yourself on the line and catch a flight to corporate headquarters to plead your case. "So, profits are too low," you begin. "Let's solve the right problem. Let's look at *why* they're too low. Are our costs too high for the margins we expect? Let's look at why our costs are too high. Are sales volumes low? Why are they low? Let's talk to our sales force and see what they think. Are our material costs out of control? Why? Let's investigate alternative sources. Is production inefficient? Why? Let's talk to our assembly people. Is our facility too large? Why? Do we really need all this space? Perhaps our facility is too small. Let's examine whether there might be economies of scale. Are our research and new product development costs out-of-control? Why? Let's take a closer look at what's going on. Do we need to cut our prices to compete? Let's find out what our competition is really charging and what they offer that we don't. Also, have we considered how our customers may view this? Might they take this as a sign that all is not well with us?"

All you accomplished by putting yourself on the line and speaking your mind was that you got upper management thinking, especially when you mentioned that you'd recently read that the majority of companies going through cuts of this nature do not achieve their desired results. In fact, you told them that a downward spiral in revenue and profits often follows.

The end result was that you were told the decision had already been made. You got back on a plane bound for home feeling frustrated. Your opinion had fallen on deaf ears, and there was nothing you could do but what you were told to do. All you can do now is sit back and watch what happens.

You try to put yourself in the position of upper management knowing they must answer to a Board of Directors and the company's stockholders. You realized that with profits having been low, the temptation to cut was there. But you knew what the consequences would be in your branch—these cuts would decrease your ability to maintain production and provide quality service. You thought about the expensive termination payoffs. You said to yourself, "Some way to cut costs—paying someone for many months not to work!" You thought about the insecurity and uncertainty that would be felt by those who remained and worried that some of your valuable intellectual property might walk out the door. You knew cuts were usually done at branch levels because it's often easier that way, but they're cutting the very people who are most visible to customers and who provide the best chances of beating the competition. How could they have grossly underestimated the personal relationships these people have with our customers?

You shudder to think what might happen if an entire business account might follow a disgruntled terminee who might suddenly become a star performer for the competition. What if your employees get angry enough to attack your company through its existing customers just to prove a point—or worse, to get revenge? Why didn't they make cuts at corporate headquarters and empower your branch to operate more autonomously? "That's the way it is in today's real world," you tell yourself. A deep sigh comes from your gut, and you think about how your people are going to respond to this dreaded announcement.

Can you relate to how this person felt? As a branch manager, he worked long hours for five hard years, traveled extensively to seek new business, provided quality training for his team, and significantly increased profitability in his branch. Then he was forced to make cutbacks that set back his entire operation. If you can relate to how he felt when this occurred, then it shouldn't surprise you to learn that he's now a sales manager for a competitor.

My neighbor Carl was told by his senior vice-president, "As part of the recent merger, you've been assigned the task of recommending which thirty people from your department should be offered a job with the new organization, and which twenty will have to find new jobs."

Carl's wife told me that during the three weeks this was going on, he didn't sleep a wink. A few weeks later, I bumped into him in our parking garage and chatted with him. "I'm glad I still have a job, but I feel horrible," he said. "I've been with some of these people for years, and I had to give them the ax."

"How did you select those who stayed?" I asked.

"I offered jobs to whomever I thought would perform most effectively, and would make me and my VP look good in the new organization."

Or perhaps you know someone like Cheryl, a dynamic financial analyst with a master's degree who worked for a major telecommunications company. She excelled at her job, but was about to experience "burnout" from the mental strain of her work and the long hours the job demanded. When the company merged with another big player, she was one of the few people in her department who was selected to stay on with the new company. They told her they wanted her to work in the new organization because they considered her to be a "star" performer. She also learned that she would have to relocate if she wanted the position.

She accepted their offer and they moved her to another state, away from her family and life-long friends. There she found herself surrounded by other "stars"—young people with master's degrees, who were, like her, overworked, achievement-oriented people. Her new manager gave her the impression that he was scrambling to make the merger work and keep the decision-makers happy. She was apprehensive about the new organization but was pacified by remembering the considerable pay increase that came with the position.

About six months later, Cheryl came back to Chicago to visit. I asked her, "How are you adjusting to the new job and the new culture?"

What she told me came as no surprise considering she is working for a powerful corporation who merged with another equally powerful one. "All the employees who retained their jobs are expected to work long hours. We're paid well, but management drives us hard and puts many demands on us. Within four months, three of my colleagues quit because they couldn't take the pressure. When I expressed my concerns to upper-level management that others would eventually quit for the same reason I was told, 'We want only *stars* in our new organization. Don't be concerned. Now that we know who can take the heat and who can't, we'll relax a little.' "

The last I heard, though, she told me things have not lightened up but have gotten worse. Now, she's surrounded by "superstars" who've raised the performance bar. I hope she can take it.

These are only some of the realities of today's world but, of course, not everyone is in situations like these. I work with many enlightened organizations that truly value their people as much as they value their customers. These smart companies listen to employee ideas as well as train, involve, and reward them for performance. They strive to develop a reputation as an "Employer of Choice"—a company everyone wants to work for. They realize that in a tight job market, retaining quality employees and treating them well is crucial to their long-term success. They implement programs that both enhance business performance and meet increasingly diverse workforce expectations. This is wise because, as I remind decision-makers time and again in my presentations, "It's your *people* who will or will not carry your organization successfully into the future."

I encourage employers to remember that every person in their company is a player in gaining a competitive advantage, especially if they're in a market where products and services are basically the same. More often then not, it's the people in their firms who make them different, even unique. In the highest-tech industries, smart companies know it's their people who drive quality and customer-satisfaction, and create the long-term relationships that lead to customer loyalty, growth, and profit.

No matter what your circumstances, you may be one of thousands of people in this country who feel overwhelmed by the demands of the work place. The speed of change, the new technology you must learn, the competitors you must outsmart, and lack of life-balance are all daily challenges you must face. This is why I believe that maintaining the right frame of mind and keeping things in the right perspective can be more important than any other skill you've honed or technique you've applied. If you lose your perspective, you can't be effective in today's environment.

Because we've looked at the reality of living and working in today's real world, it may make sense, therefore, to take a good, hard look inside ourselves before we discuss concepts and techniques on how to beat the competition. You may need to overcome what could be your biggest competitor—yourself! In other words, if the title of this book is *Wake Up and Smell the Competition,* this is the "wake up" part of the book. Call it self-awareness, self-discovery, a kick-start. Call it what you like.

Since the age of eight, I've played the violin and from Day One, I learned that a violin must first be properly tuned before it can be played. If it is not, the result will be sour notes, even if you're a virtuoso. The same holds true in the business world. Your thinking may need to be properly tuned before you can learn and implement the strategies and techniques we will address. I hope this section will help give your mind that tune-up if it needs one. If it doesn't, you may gain some insight on what type of mindset people need to make it in today's world.

Chapter 1

Three Types of People ...
Which Are You?

Based on what I've observed about human nature, I'm convinced that the type of person you choose to be will determine your level of success, and your ability to compete and WIN. I long ago concluded that there are basically three types of people in this world:

- Slackers
- Coasters
- Achievers

As we examine the characteristics of each, think of yourself, the people in your company—your employees, customers and coworkers, and also the people in your personal life. See if you agree with me.

The Slackers

You know who they are, although you might call them by less-flattering names—especially if your company employs them. They're the moaners, groaners, gripers, nit-pickers, complainers, dream-busters and mopes of this world. Sound like a great group, don't they? They all belong to the same group—the "Happy Being Miserable Club." I call them Slackers because they go through the motions of their job, but lack initiative and involvement. If there's a problem, they wait for someone else to fix it or worse, say, "Told you so!"

As far as being open to new methods of doing things or new ideas, their minds are set in concrete. Slackers don't care about their own productivity and if something falls through the cracks, it's always someone else's fault. (I bet you're already thinking of someone with these characteristics. If you're a manager, you'd probably like to know right now how to get rid of them! You'll find that information in Section 2.)

As far as Slackers are concerned, negativity drives their lives. When they go home at night, they complain about their customers, their jobs, their bosses, and the traffic. Then they park themselves in front of the TV and tune out the rest of the world. When it comes to making plans for their future, they simply don't because they're stuck wherever they are, which is usually in their own minds. They consider themselves "victims" of whomever or whatever. Sadly, they don't realize that thinking of themselves as victims of their world keeps them feeling oppressed and holds them back from professional accomplishment and personal happiness.

Slackers are people who don't take risks, and who walk backwards so they'll never stub a toe. They usually believe and accept the fate of their own negative prophecies. Then, they deny the fact that they themselves have taken a pessimistic stance in life, and in so doing, consider themselves as "have-nots." They react negatively whenever they see positive people who are doing something with their lives. If they devoted as much time to getting things done as they did to sitting on the fence sniping at others, the world would be a very different place. It's much easier to say, "No, it can't be done," than to say, "What do we have to do to make it happen?" They see challenges as obstacles, not as steppingstones.

They're the ones who don't see the value of marketing the company's products on the Internet, and say the company's new restructuring will fail. They're the ones who resist learning new systems or software and tell customers, "Sorry, but we just can't do that." They're the ones who see how a strategy can be improved, but prefer to complain about its failure to their friends at lunch. They're the ones who feel that, because they're union workers, they can't easily be fired so they slack off on the job. If they see a piece of paper on the floor, they'd say, "We might get a paper cut if we picked it up." I'm sure you're beginning to see the picture, although Slackers would certainly say the picture is faded!

Slackers *major in the minors* throughout their lives because they expect things to be handed to them. They're unwilling to work hard to get what they want. They even feel sorry for themselves for having to work to make a living. You often hear them expressing envy over those who are wealthy. "It must be nice," they say. This attitude holds them back even more because they feel that they're not wealthy, and this is why they can't become successful. You may hear them refer to a successful person as "lucky." They complain and focus on everything that's wrong and are considered to be "negaholics." The only time these "Princes and Princesses of Pessimism" aren't complaining is when they're asleep. These poor unfortunate souls need a lot of help to get out of the rut they keep themselves in by their obvious inexperience in feeling positive about anything. I've often felt they became this way because they were raised in a negative environment, or that maybe they actually enjoy going through life thinking of themselves as victims. I've also observed that they associate with others who are like themselves, hence the old saying: "Misery loves company."

I wonder what has happened to them in their pasts to make them such pessimists. Maybe one of the many prohibitions they learned at an early age was an unspoken rule: "Don't have fun; don't enjoy life." If that's the type of upbringing they had, it's made them martyrs, people who will not let themselves embrace the pleasures of day-to-day living. Maybe they associate struggling through each day with this type of attitude with some sort of sainthood.

In your personal life, Slackers are people I encourage you to avoid because whenever your paths cross, they'll pull you and everyone else down and zap your energy. Worst of all, they usually don't realize they're doing it.

Avoiding Slackers in the work place is not always possible. If you're in a leadership position or are a member of a self-directed work team, I urge you to quickly confront them about their negativity or employee morale will diminish and productivity will suffer. In Section 3, we'll see how to tactfully approach this type of person.

The Coasters

Unlike the Slackers, our next group does not so dramatically impact others. I call them "Coasters" because they seem to "coast" through their lives.

On the job, the Coasters are punctual, knowledgeable, and responsible. They do what is required and expected of them, but rarely display any real initiative. They may feel strongly about something but usually prefer not to make waves. When they get a flash of inspiration or an original idea that may give their company or themselves better results, they rarely act on it because they're content with the status quo and are quite satisfied right where they are.

In their personal lives, I have observed that Coasters go home from work and usually stick to a familiar routine. They like going to the same places and doing the same things. There's nothing really wrong with this, but I feel that because they're not adventurous, they often settle for a life of mediocrity. I believe if you approach life tentatively, you reap only a portion of its gifts. The Coasters of this world may be living their lives in gray tones when they could be living them in vibrant Technicolor. Could it be that some might simply lack the courage to let the colors emerge—to feel them, absorb them, and be inspired by them? Unfortunately, they may never achieve any great accomplishments because they're comfortable where they are.

When faced with any type of change in their jobs or their lives, they don't always respond well, or may even be complacent. I believe this is because they don't like leaving their comfort zone. They're content to meet the company sales quota every month. They expect no more and no less of themselves. They get in on time, take their coffee breaks, and leave on time regardless of customer commitments. They'll politely fix any problems a customer brings to them, but will rarely proactively contact a customer to find out how the product is working. They're content with their merit raises, and neither complain about nor expect promotions, bonuses or "exceptional" performance ratings. They will agreeably attend training seminars, but rarely look for ways to apply what they've learned.

See what I mean about "coasting? A little "excitement" in their lives might do them some good. Perhaps if they'd only look for it, they'd find it. Think of the Coasters you know, and you may agree that they comprise the largest number of the three groups. When I discuss the Coasters in my seminars, people often raise their hands and comment, "All too many people I manage are Coasters—how do I handle them?" and, "Sometimes people become Coasters because they've gotten shot down too often."

Can a Coaster compete and win? Yes! Everyone has the ability to beat the competition, but the Coasters of this world need external motivation, a strong leader to encourage them and keep them on track.

Sadly for most Coasters, if they don't receive proper coaching, they may never reach their full potential. They may never win that big account, get that promotion, or win over a difficult customer.

The Achievers

The "Achievers" are the true masters of excellence. They make great salespeople, successful entrepreneurs, superb managers, and excellent customer service people. They tend to achieve success in whatever they do, not only because of their natural competitive spirit and enthusiasm, but because they set their goals higher than others and they accomplish them.

Achievers make great leaders because *they encourage others* to achieve. They manage to focus on the positive in everyone they encounter and bring out the best in others because they know that doing so benefits everyone in many untold ways. Being in the same room can easily transmit their positive energy to others. Positive attitude and determination are the ammunition they use to get what they want. They know that a positive mindset combined with the energy they put into their work determines their own and others' success.

Achievers know that to be able to compete and win in today's real world, risk-taking supported by rationale can be a strong force of unlimited potential. Once they get a creative idea, make a decision or commit to anything, they put forth extraordinary effort. They're thirsty for new ideas and anxious to try them out. They thrive on challenge because they love that great feeling of having conquered a difficult task, of landing a new account, or participating in a successful team project. After attending a seminar, they head back to the office and implement the ideas they've learned.

Achievers maintain a positive attitude and don't let negative situations bother them, even when they're the last people at the baggage claim area of the airport. Mistakes or disappointments of the past do not cause them to agonize, for they realize that obstacles and difficulties are part of everyone's life and are there to be overcome. They view these as opportunities for advancement and increased self-awareness, and find joy in facing them and coming out on top.

Unlike Coasters, a life of mediocrity rarely exists for them. They're always trying new things and striving to figure out what it takes to elevate their success. They consistently strive to be more than they are and perform at their highest level at the most crucial times. Achievers are adept at acquiring whatever skills they need, but their true edge comes from making each accomplishment or victory spur them to greater ambition. And Achievers always accept full responsibility for their actions and choices in life.

Achievers have learned to love what they do, and always do their best because their values dictate that they must. That's why, today, every company wants them. They're the people who set new records for sales because they've learned to maximize their personal productivity. They arrive early in the morning, stay late when needed, yet make time for a personal life. They will not only correct a problem for a customer and exceed customer expectations but will recommend what action the company can take to prevent the problem from recurring. They are eager for the next promotion, and understand that hard work and commitment bring recognition to their leadership qualities.

Achievers should not be confused with "Overachievers" who are obsessed with work, drive everyone else crazy, have no personal balance, and are in bad need of that Twelve Step Program, "Overachievers Anonymous." I've known some Overachievers who seem to lust after money, power, and glory at the expense of their well-being, and may even be called "Achievement Addicts." They hesitate to take a vacation because they're afraid they might miss some action. These individuals may be perfectionists with impossibly high standards. What makes them difficult is they expect everyone to be like them. Industrial psychologists often find that these dysfunctional people immerse themselves in their work so they can cut themselves off from feeling any type of emotion.

When I think of the Overachievers I have known, I believe they've become obsessed with overwork because, spiritually, they're running on empty. Interestingly, the few Overachievers I have known who, for one reason or another (usually a warning from their doctor) did recognize they had a problem and sought balance in their lives, found that ambition did not have to disappear entirely from their lives. They also found that good health, balance and peacefulness are must-haves to avoid job burnout. The cemetery is full of those who never slowed down their life-threatening pace. If you're an Overachiever, quickly read Section 4 before it's too late.

The Achievers, in contrast, are enthusiastic about their work and their personal lives. They've learned the importance of having direction and goals in life, and personal balance as well. They've learned to love their work, yet they're not all-consumed by it nor do they expect themselves to be perfect. In fact, when they make a mistake, they laugh about it.

Besides the obvious, other reasons companies want Achievers in their workforce is that most are professional and ethical at all times and rarely focus on achieving at the expense of others. They don't want their peers to lose while they're winning—success is not a zero sum game to them. They help their colleagues and companies succeed, which is why companies who look to attract, develop, and retain Achievers offer profit-sharing and stock-purchase plans, along with wellness and child care programs, as we'll see in Section 2.

Let's not forget to pay tribute to a very special class of Achiever—the entrepreneur. I believe that all entrepreneurs are Achievers because they have the ultimate commitment. As entrepreneurs, they put a great deal on the line. Often they operate on blind faith—moving forward even though they don't know where their next buck is coming from. They accept responsibility for the livelihood of their employees, and many tell me how they worry about their employees' families. Indeed, they're in a class by themselves.

What a group! We need more Achievers to sell our products, start new companies, head up teams, volunteer in the community, service customers, and inspire the Coasters to be more than they are. "Where are they? Show me!" you say. The answer lies ahead.

People often tell me they believe there is some crossover; that people can be Achievers at work yet struggle through their personal lives. Perhaps so, but with thought, you may agree that most people fall into the same trap. If they're negative in the workplace, a Slacker, they usually also whine about their personal life. Their relationships provide very little value to their partners, families and friends. You may also find that the Coasters, who stay in boring and unfulfilling jobs, usually don't like to take risks in their personal lives either. Often they stay in unfulfilling relationships or hang on to relationships with people who no longer provide value in their lives.

When it comes to having a competitive spirit, most Slackers don't. If they happen to be one of those few who participate in sports, say tennis or golf, they focus on what they did wrong and gnash their teeth over it long after the game is over. They do the same in business. The Coasters are often afraid to acknowledge their competitive side, and may give up before the game begins. The Achievers keep playing until they finally win.

To sum up the difference between these three groups, let's use this book as an example. If you gave Slackers a copy of this book, they would protest that they don't have time to read it and complain that you've just given them something more to do. Coasters would thank you for the book, look at the cover, skim a few chapters and then put it on a bookshelf. Achievers would thank you for the book, read it to get the most they could from it and then thank you again for sharing it with them. Then, they would implement each idea or skill they could use.

So if these are the three the types of people in this world, how do you see yourself? If you're a Slacker, you're probably not reading this book anyway. Unless you transform your life, your attitude will keep you feeling oppressed. Only *you* hold the key to your freedom and your success. Stop waiting for someone or something to give you what it is that you need; quit complaining, and take responsibility for yourself. If you do, the door of opportunity will swing wide open for you. When it does, walk through it—no charge!

If you're a Coaster, you have hopefully begun your "awakening" and are beginning to see that you may want more out of your professional and personal life. To you, I recommend that you experiment. Try something new. Try stepping out. You may have held yourself back for too long. Assume responsibility for your career and circumstances. Yes, you'll make mistakes but from those mistakes you will grow. You may unmask life-enriching abilities you never knew you had. Make a decision to get out there and test the waters to see how much better you can make your job and your life.

If you're an Achiever, you may want to skim the next chapter because you're already practicing a positive attitude and are in the right frame of mind to WIN! If you're looking for positive reinforcement, however, do read it. Finally, if you're a leader who wants to know how to deal with the Slackers in this world and inspire the Coasters, you'll find useful information in Sections 2 and 3.

Chapter 2

Haven't We Heard Enough About Positive Attitude?

W e've all heard enough about positive attitude. If you feel the same as I do, you can skip this chapter ... but at your own risk. Keep in mind that, according to a Stanford Research Institute study, success is 88 percent attitude and 12 percent education. I'm sure it still holds true because positive attitude is an important factor in your ability to get what you want in life ... and stay sane while getting it. It's also a topic of great importance to my clients.

When senior level executives book me for a speaking engagement, I always ask them what message they want me to "drive home" at their meeting or conference. Most will ask me to address the importance of providing quality customer service, establishing customer loyalty, achieving excellence in sales, and being able to "think outside the box." (I'm so tired of these buzzwords and phrases. Aren't you?) But most important, they say, is talking about positive attitude. These senior leaders recognize that maintaining a positive attitude is critical because it's obvious that positive people are happy people, and happy people create a positive image for the company. They also want me to talk about it because there are usually a number of Coasters and Slackers in their organizations who need a wake up call.

Even the most sophisticated business professionals and executives need a boost once in a while—a positive attitude shot in the arm to keep them fired up. The reason is obvious. In today's real world, people work longer hours and are being told to "do more with less." (How I dislike that phrase!)

The workplace pressure to perform seems endless. Perhaps sales are down, budgets have been cut, or they have experienced downsizing and restructuring. Their stress level is high and life-balance is low, so their attitudes are not consistently upbeat. That's the reality of today's world and is why many managers seek ways to give their people a jumpstart.

If you're a sales professional, please consider this: a recent national survey examined why salespeople fail. You would think it would most often be because of high prices or poor quality. But 15 percent of the respondents attributed failure to "poor training," another 15 percent said "poor management" and another 20 percent said "poor communication skills." A full 50 percent, however, said that salespeople fail because of "lack of positive attitude."

So, what is positive attitude anyway? Is it simply thinking about positive outcomes? Again, no. That's too simplistic. As you read on, I hope you'll open your mind to a different way of thinking about what constitutes positive attitude.

Love What You Do

Positive attitude is not only about choosing to have a good outlook about any given situation, but also about learning to love what you do. I have observed that outstanding business people are successful because they deeply love their work. As we mentioned earlier, the Achievers of this world know that if you can learn to love your job, you'll be more productive, more creative, and more content. Think of most successful people you know, and you may agree that most are passionate about what they do, are rarely affected by negativity, and tend to work harder than others. I know for certain that the better your attitude, the harder you work. And the wonderful truth is, the harder you work, the "luckier" you get.

But what if you don't love what you do? What if you own your own company and no longer feel the excitement and enthusiasm you had when you first started the business? What if you can't take the pressures of being an entrepreneur and no longer find joy in your business? Then maybe it's time to get out. If this is the case, you'll need a booster shot of positive attitude to realize that you can take what you've learned from one business and be successful in another, like those in our next chapter have done.

What if you have a job you don't love? What can you do if you're bored and feel there's no chance for advancement or opportunity? Those with a positive attitude have the mind-set that if they have a job they don't enjoy, it may be a steppingstone to something greater. If you have an Achiever attitude, you will do your best no matter what because of who you are. It's about taking what you've got right now and making the best of it. It's starting up a little side business if you don't want to quit your fulltime job. It's also being positive enough to summon up the courage to ask for a better position. You'll learn the *right* way to ask in Section 3.

Ann and Greg are both are sales trainers for a prominent insurance company. Both had ambitions to move up the career ladder in the training department. Both were talented and deserving of a promotion. In the training department, there was often a shifting of resources, restructuring of teams, people transferring in and people transferring out. Finally, Greg got frustrated with the constant change. He felt he was overdue for a promotion, and began to lose focus and felt dejected about his future. Greg, though, never complained to his peers nor did the quality of his work suffer.

But in fact, Greg was really an Achiever who allowed himself to become a victim of a negative attitude. He decided to take a lateral transfer to a different department with limited promotional opportunities, mostly because he'd become discouraged by all the training department's uncertainty.

Ann, on the other hand, kept a positive attitude about the changes. She felt that, if she kept trying her best and displayed an enthusiastic attitude, then eventually her opportunity would come. If someone transferred in at a higher position, she would ask herself, "What qualities and skills does this person have that I don't?" Then she would read books, attend seminars and read articles available on the Internet to help her acquire those skills. Eventually, Ann got the position she was looking for.

But what about Greg? He did fine in his new department but eventually realized that he had no higher job opportunities there. He ended up returning to a position in the training department—to the same position he had when he left. Sadly, had he stayed where his skills were best suited, he, too, would have had his desired promotion.

Don't get me wrong—there's absolutely nothing wrong with transferring departments or changing companies. People do it all the time for a better opportunity. In Greg's case it was a question

of doing it for the right reasons. He wasn't transferring departments because he was running to something better, but was running from something he perceived was worse when, in reality, it
wasn't. His allowed a negative attitude to hold back his professional development.

Believe

When I'm asked what breeds success in sales, management,
entrepreneurship, customer relations or whatever, I say, "There's
no single, mystical, magical secret to success ... but you must
believe." Positive attitude is about believing in your company, in its
products or services, and in yourself. It's also about making the
customer feel your belief from your words and actions. It means
explaining to your subordinates that reorganization in the company
is necessary, even when you (as manager) might not personally reap
the benefits. It means believing that you'll make that next sale, even
though you lost the last two. Without this type of mindset, how can
you possibly dream to compete?

Although you can exercise absolute control over very little of
what occurs in your life; the attitude with which you choose to greet
the day, approach a situation or respond to people is fully within
your control. Your attitude about any condition, present or future, is
within your power to choose.

Come to Grips with the Day-to-Day Challenges

Did you ever have a bad day when nothing goes right, and you
wanted to just say, "Hey, to hell with it all!"? You want to give it all
up and quit trying. If you're like most people, you probably get that
feeling more often than you care to admit. We all tend to get frustrated at times. Positive attitude, though, means coming to grips
with life's everyday challenges: the sale that fell through, rush hour
traffic, that lost promotion, the encounter with the customer from
hell, the close-minded boss, equipment failures, delayed or can-
celed flights, or lost luggage. We all face these everyday irritants
and frustrations, so why choose to let yourself get aggravated by
these disappointments? As one of my friends says, "These are merely
some of life's "inconveniences."

Sure, it's okay to get irritated once in a while—we're only human, but you certainly don't want to keep stress bottled up inside. Part of having a positive attitude is letting disappointments fall off your shoulders quickly. Focusing your attention incessantly on challenging situations that agitate you will *keep* you overly stressed. Obsessing over problems leaves little room for solutions. Let disappointments, lost sales and lost promotions go, and move forward with the momentum of positive attitude. Forget the "pity me" attitude and go with the "watch me!" attitude. You have to say, "That's life. I've got to learn to roll with the punches, and keep on pitching." Then, look to the future with positive expectations, and expect to WIN!

Achieve control of your attitude and emotions with precision thinking and acting. Psych yourself to stay focused on winning with the spirited mentality of a sprinter combined with the perseverance and endurance of a marathon runner. Each day starts new and with it comes new opportunity. Don't surrender your spirit, but if you do, you might try this: Allow yourself to be down for only that day. Feel sorry for yourself as much as you want but promise yourself that the moment the sun rises the next day, you'll greet it with a positive attitude! Then discipline yourself to do it. Remember that you bring your attitude to your job and to your friends and family each day.

Attitude: Is It Really Everything?

We often hear the term "attitude is everything." I disagree. You could say that attitude is really what helps give you an edge. You can even say that attitude is at the center, but it's not everything. I believe that knowing your strengths and weaknesses are also important.

Many people dream of being professional athletes, movie stars or recording artists. They can have the greatest belief in themselves, but if they don't have the talent, they're setting themselves up for disappointment.

If you're 5' 2" and 30 pounds overweight and have never dribbled a basketball in your life, let's be honest, all the positive attitude in the world isn't going to help you beat the talent of a Michael Jordan in a one-on-one basketball game. Where you have natural ability is where you want to develop your skills. You need to recognize where you do not have the innate ability or capacity, and then move on. I'm not encouraging you to give up on a dream just because it may be difficult to attain. Some of the most rewarding successes in life come from overcoming barriers. You need to balance your devotion and optimism with realism and recognize that, wherever you may be lacking in skill, you'll need to work hard to develop your competence.

Let's say you want to be promoted to a management position. You already possess solid analytical skills and forecasting abilities, but you know that you're a soft-spoken person who doesn't like confrontation. Rather than thinking your technical abilities will be enough to get you the promotion, recognize that you'll need training and practice in leadership, communication, conflict resolution, and probably several other skills. It's critical to know where your competency lies, and where you need help if you want to acquire new abilities or develop latent talents. Keep in mind that your strengths have gotten you where you are, but also be mindful that your weaknesses may stop you from going where you want to go.

Business professionals who are Achievers fully understand that a positive and optimistic view of life is essential for continued success, but they also know that a positive attitude should never be allowed to distort the truth. They can see the reality of any given situation, analyze it, but do so in a positive context.

Beverly was a sales manager in a financial services company whose sales were down for three consecutive quarters. She knew her brokers were the backbone of the organization, and she supported them accordingly, remaining optimistic that they would turn things around. Beverly, though, didn't let her positive attitude keep her from seeing the truth; sales weren't likely to turn around unless the company changed its sales strategy.

Many of their competitors had begun to offer financial services on the Internet, and even though the president of the company was very traditional, Beverly recognized that if the company was going to survive, they would have to follow suit. She began to map out a strategy that would strengthen both the traditional broker channel and start up a brand new Internet channel. Beverly then developed a strategy designed to persuade the president into accepting this new approach.

Beverly and others like her are "solution-focused," not "problem-focused." They keep things in proper perspective when they handle challenges or obstacles so they can envision positives and possibilities rather than negatives or limitations. It's clear to me from observing Achievers that much of their success lies in the fact that they invariably possess the ability to think clearly, critically and objectively without becoming either blindly optimistic or unreasonably negative.

Here's another example of what can occur in today's real world and why positive attitude is not everything. One of my clients told me about a meeting that was run by one of the best managers he ever knew. This great leader conducted what he called a "Blue Skies" meeting. All the sales people gathered in a room for two days and analyzed how they were performing, where they felt the company should be headed, what the opposition was up to and what new products could really beat the competition. He told me this wise manager analyzed what was needed to beat the competition by listening to field input, and together they identified what the company needed to do to ensure a more successful future.

Everyone left the meeting feeling positive, energized, and hopeful that management would respond to his or her suggestions. After the CFO analyzed what funds were required to implement their ideas, management informed them that their plan was rejected as not economically feasible. All the power the group felt after walking out of that great meeting was lost. The manager felt the same frustration his team felt. The company wasn't willing to take the financial risk business that growth often requires. It took the sales team a long time to bounce back. In situations such as this, maintaining a positive attitude is difficult, but recognize that you must learn to accept decisions over which you have no control.

Remember that a positive attitude is not "everything" because it can't guarantee success. Every Achiever has been defeated in certain endeavors, but look to an outstanding quarterback who learns why he was defeated and works with his coach to create a new game plan for the next game. Positive attitude alone cannot replace hard work, talent, knowledge, interpersonal skills and old-fashioned perseverance. What it does do is fuel a "can-do" attitude, which is something we need to be able to compete and win. It's also the foundation for growth and forward movement, and generates *personal happiness*—the ultimate measure of success.

Stay Young

One last thing about positive attitude is that it's a lot like anti-wrinkle cream. Although it's not exactly a fountain of youth, it can make you feel younger. A recent survey conducted by *Prevention* magazine found that people with positive attitudes said they looked and felt younger than their age. In fact, they were even told by others that they looked younger than they were. If that isn't a good reason to stay positive, I don't know what is! By the way, want a face-lift in ten seconds? Smile. You'll not only look younger and feel better, but you'll make everyone else around you feel better, too.

Chapter 3

Be a Chameleon

One of the most intriguing places I have ever visited is the richly colorful island continent of Australia. Several years ago, I took a much-needed vacation in "Oz" (as the natives call it) and promised myself I wouldn't think about business the entire trip. With its wealth of tropical rain forests, rivers, mountains, and sandy beaches, Australia is ruggedly beautiful and wildly romantic. Who would want to think about business in such a place? What I loved most was the wildlife—the koalas, wombats, lizards, kangaroos and splendid tropical birds. I still have visions of flocks of parakeets, white cockatoos and pink galas flying freely and gracefully through the trees. What a beautiful sight! I truly felt as one with nature.

One day, while lying in the hot sun near the beach, I saw a reptile a little over one foot long poke its head out of the foliage nearby. As it moved forward, I almost thought I might be seeing things. The animal blended so well with the foliage that I could barely make out its shape. My eyes stayed focused on the creature and as it moved from under the green shrubbery on to the sand, I was amazed to see its greenish color slowly change to a brownish haze. Then I realized, "Of course! It's a chameleon!" It wasn't, however, like the three-inch creatures we see running around in Florida and the Caribbean. This was one big lizard! I found out later from a zoologist friend that this species is called a "cryptic" chameleon.

Even though I'd promised myself to not think of business while on vacation, I couldn't resist thinking of one of my seminars, "The Chameleon: Leading Through Change." There I was, in one of the most beautiful places on earth, pondering my thoughts about the chameleon and the business lesson it teaches us. When its environment changes, the chameleon effortlessly changes with it. Its biological success lies in its ability to rapidly adapt to changes in its environment, fluidly matching its pigmentation to its surroundings. Put it on a rock and it turns brown. Put it on a leaf and it turns green. Because of its ability to respond to change, the chameleon is the perfect example of adaptability.

Unfortunately, the same cannot be said for us humans. Whether we're going through a merger or acquisition, are required to adhere to a new policy or procedure, need to learn a new computer system, or find a new job, most of us are basically resistant to change. Humans are creatures of habit. We function best when we follow a fairly regular schedule and welcome the contentment of our routines. A set method of operating keeps us feeling secure. Change takes us out of the familiar and into the unfamiliar. It can make us uncomfortable, challenge the way we view ourselves, dampen a positive attitude, disrupt our lives and force us to face disconcerting uncertainty. People feel warm and protected in their comfort zones. Like moths to a light, they're drawn to the familiar, even though they fail to recognize that the object of their attraction offers them no real security or sustenance.

You hear their familiar refrains every day: "There's no way I'm going to transfer to that department," "I don't like that new accounting software. The old one was better," "I'm not going to tell my customers we're changing our invoicing procedures," "I don't know why we're going through all that rigmarole to get certified with that association," "Doing a competitive analysis is a waste of my time," and "Telling our customers to order our products from our web site instead of our catalog is foolish." Sound familiar?

As I said, we've all heard plenty of messages about how the rate of change is accelerating, and how we must be adaptable to change if we're to survive in this world. This is especially true given the advances of computer technology, for the futurists tell us that we'll soon be using technology we can't even imagine today. Many people will be working in jobs that are yet to be invented. For many of us, the pace and scope of such changes is accelerating toward a seemingly unmanageable hyper-speed. Organizations in all industries are rethinking their entire business strategies and making fast changes to keep up with the demands of today's more sophisticated customer and trying to get a jump on the competition. That's why we hear so much about how we must accept change, as well as the old adage, "Change is inevitable—growth is optional."

I'm probably not telling you anything you don't already know, but here's a perspective I find that many employees fail to consider: When organizations change, they do so to be able to compete more effectively in the marketplace. Organizational changes then, require that you and everyone else to adapt in order to fit into the new organization. People, however, are motivated to change by the same reasons as organizations. For the most part, people adapt in order to keep their jobs with the company. They aren't thinking about competing in the marketplace or positioning the organization to succeed. They simply want to get through the change so that their lives can become more comfortable again. This is no way to get ahead of the competition.

As an Achiever, you need to think of change as more than that. If you're not adaptable to change, it may seriously impede your ability to compete and hold you back from making a decision to be a WINNER in spite of the change. Charles Darwin taught us about "survival of the fittest"—that only the strongest survive. That's as true in the business world as it is in the animal world. For today's business professionals, those who are the most flexible and adaptable to change will not only survive but also thrive in a changing world. I call this, "Survival of the Finest in the 21st Century."

So if you want to WIN, you must not only embrace and learn from change and become like the chameleon, but you need to initiate it as well. What we need now is to promote and initiate change proactively—not reactively. Lead … don't follow. This is never easy but you can, and must, if you want to stay "ahead of the curve."

Reinvent

Now, I'm not advocating that anyone to leave his or her company, but I've always felt that if you're really unhappy with your job, you'll be doing yourself and your company a favor by going somewhere else. Perhaps you're thinking of a career change, or need inspiration from those who have done so to inspire you to take a new position. What better example of being able to adapt to change than those who've given up the security of their current job and boldly tried something new. Some of the most fascinating people

I've met are those who have courageously moved from one career to another:

- My friend Tim was a drummer in a rock band. He worked in clubs six days a week. One day, he decided he couldn't take the smoke and the late hours anymore, so he took a job selling automobile parts. Ten years later, he became vice president of Sales and Marketing at a Fortune 100 manufacturing company.

- My high school friend Ed dreamed of becoming a celebrated photographer but was devastated to learn to learn he was color-blind. Rather than letting disappointment discourage his dreams for a successful future, he turned his life toward a career in sales. He eventually became a regional sales manager for a Fortune 500 company.

- My friend Photini came to this country from Greece at the age of seventeen. She had only a few dollars in her pocket and no command of the English language. She adapted and made her way. She graduated college with a degree in computer science and was one of the first women to become a computer programmer. She did exceptionally well in her career with Hewlett Packard, but wanted to pursue her true love—race horses. She left the company and became one of the most renowned breeders of thoroughbreds in the state of Illinois.

- My friend Gayle Olson owned a delicatessen. Even though her business was a cash cow, she simply got sick of making sandwiches. At age 40, she sold her store, earned her college degree, and found fulfillment as a radiology technician.

- Gayle's brother-in-law, Sam, was a chiropractor with a thriving practice. When he injured his shoulder, he could no longer adjust his patients' vertebrae. Not letting that discourage him, he shifted his focus in another direction. He founded a company that provides laundry services to major hotels and hospitals, and achieved success in a completely different business.

- Ian Lewis was a school teacher who loved to teach. Unlike some of his colleagues who had grown to hate teaching and felt trapped and unqualified do anything else, Ian was excited to try something new. He left the classroom to join one of the top management-consulting firms in the country. Today, he is a training manager at a Fortune 100 insurance company.

- One of my mentors, Dr. John Powers, was a professor in communications. While teaching was very rewarding to him, as with Ian Lewis, he yearned for something more, and became a successful playwright, author and one of the country's top motivational speakers.

- The late Congressman Sonny Bono is a noteworthy example of someone who was able to adapt to new circumstances in different stages of his life and be successful in all of them. His career moved from a musician, to a restaurant manager, to international celebrity entertainer, to being a mayor and, finally, a congressman.

- Michael Dell was a premed student at the University of Texas who built his own computer. Friends began to ask him to build computers for them and business snowballed. He soon realized that making computers excited him more than medicine, so he left the premed program to pursue his passion and ultimately became one of the richest men in Texas.

If all these people could completely "reinvent" themselves and make major career changes, then certainly you should be able to change the things that aren't working for you. Although none of them arrived at their destinations overnight, and all experienced a great deal of uncertainty during the transition period, they eventually found fulfillment in their new profession.

Of course, not all of us are cut out to completely change direction in our careers, but we can be adaptable. We must look upon change as the force that causes personal and professional growth. Whether you are changing careers, learning a new system or procedure, having to participate in a self-directed work team where previously you worked autonomously, or simply changing your attitude about working with new management, change need not be dreadful. Although it *can* cause stress, it can also be rewarding and give you a sense of self-satisfaction as you conquer your new challenges.

You need to be committed to stepping forward and meeting challenges head on. No challenge is beyond your capability. Every business challenge promises wisdom and personal growth. If you make a conscious effort to embrace change, to remain flexible and adapt quickly, you can increase your odds at beating the competition. Maybe you need to change your selling or management style. If you're a business owner or executive, maybe you need to move the company in a new direction.

So, what are you prepared to change in order to beat the competition? Are you ready to use your own uniqueness in your approach to sales? Are you ready to work harder than your co-workers to get that next promotion? Are you ready to contact that intimidating prospect to get a new customer? Are you ready to help your company institute the changes brought about by the recent merger? Are you ready to create innovative ways to enhance the service you provide after the sale? Are you ready to take that challenging job in a new career, department, region, or company? Can you reinvent yourself if necessary?

Will you be like the chameleon, changing its color to adapt to a new environment, or will you be like the once big and powerful Tyrannosaurus Rex, and become extinct because you cannot respond to a changing environment? The symbolic message of the chameleon lies in its mastery of ever-changing conditions. If you choose to be like the chameleon, you may find the following helpful in your efforts to cope with the transition process.

Accept Change

Change is as continual as life. Change happens, whether we welcome it or not. When you think about it, our own lives go through the same changes as organizations; we experience restructuring, downsizing, and upsizing just like companies do. Our own little "organizations" grow when we have kids and get smaller when they move out. Perhaps a divorce causes us to go through a restructuring.

Change blows through our lives, sometimes like a gentle breeze, sometimes like a gust of wind and sometimes like a tropical storm. We may bow our heads to buck it, hoping it will blow over. We're not certain whether change is for the better. We may even experience stress and personal resistance. The point is we cannot always stop change—especially in our jobs—so we must accept it and promote it. Focus on positive opportunity change can bring and look upon it as a challenge. Encourage others to pull together for a positive result. In doing so, you will have some control over it. Change will never end until we experience that final life-ending change, and even then, life will continue on without us.

Plan

Always have a plan to implement change. Begin by setting a goal for yourself—outline the outcomes you expect. Ask yourself: "What will this change look like when it's completed?" Then, map out a strategy to get you there. For instance, if you decide you want to become a future leader in the organization, ask yourself what you must do to reach that goal. Will you need training, mentoring or experience leading smaller groups on projects? Identify those things and set a timetable for yourself.

Even if things in your life seem to change constantly, making plans will give you a stronger sense of control. If you're planning to change jobs or careers, you should also evaluate different alternatives, thus providing you with fallback options in case things change in a direction you may not have anticipated. If you wish to become an entrepreneur, recognize that hard work, hard choices, and some pain may be involved.

View Change as an Elixir

View new technology, systems, business practices and assignments as a challenge instead of an obstacle. I've already said that change may not be easy, so the attitude with which you approach it will help determine your likelihood of success. Saying, "I don't know anything about this new sales territory. This is going to be hard," is a lot different than saying, "I'm excited to learn about this new sales territory. It won't be easy learning a new customer base, but I'm anxious to see what new opportunities I can find."

Be Flexible

You may not want to change careers, but you will need to be flexible enough to work well either independently, in teams, or under direct supervision. Some people who'd hoped to have a management position find that making a lateral move is just fine and sometimes more advantageous. Successful workers and managers must be flexible enough to deal with many different environments and circumstances in today's world.

Learn to Love to Learn

Alan Toffler, the famous futurist said, "The illiterate of the future will not be those who cannot read and write, but will be those who cannot learn, unlearn, and relearn." How right he is! Have you found that, no sooner than you've mastered one type of technology, you must then learn another? Or you've just become accustomed to one procedure and then must suddenly adapt to a new one?

Achievement-oriented people know that to be able to compete, continuous learning must be a lifelong process. Learning new skills should be constant, no matter how much experience you may have and no matter how old you may be. Frank Turco, my 88 year-old uncle, is what I call an "Internet whiz." He didn't even know how to turn on a computer until he was 80! How's that for learning new skills? Focus on the sense of accomplishment you feel when you've mastered a new skill or gained knowledge on any topic.

Be Patient

Finally, be patient with yourself and others. Adapting to change doesn't happen overnight, let alone in an eight-hour workday. Keep a positive attitude and focus on the benefits and new opportunities that change can bring. Just be sure to expect a few bumps in the road along the way. When you experience stages of resistance and uncertainty but can still assimilate change and finally conquer it, you'll experience an enormous sense of accomplishment, and your self-esteem will increase.

I guess we should all envy the chameleon, for to it, change comes naturally. It needs neither training nor job aids to help it shift from brown to green and back again. We humans, on the other hand, need a little more support and guidance to make it through those uncertain times in our lives—whether it's a change in career, in mindset, in job position, or in strategy. Whether you are responsible for changing only yourself or helping an entire organization through a major change, (I'll tell you how in Section 2), the good news is that it will occur one day at a time. And that's all we have to do—take it one day at a time.

Chapter 4

Decide to Win

No matter what challenges you may be facing, I hope that, as you've been reading, you're already beginning to see a new way of looking at change and the competition—with an Achiever attitude. You'll need that first if you want to compete and win.

Secondly, you'll need a sense of vision—seeing how much more successful you can be in your present job or in a completely different career. Or, if you're an executive or manager, you'll need to have that vision first, and then see how much more successful you can make your own company, and what you can dare to accomplish.

Thirdly, you need to decide to win. This may sound strange, but winning starts with a decision. World-class athletes know that without having this type of mindset, they cannot become winners. Likewise, competitive business people know they must make a decision to win if they want to land the unattainable client, launch a new product in record time, achieve that impossible sales goal or increase productivity in their department. Making the decision to win drives your skills and performance to new levels.

As I see it, you have three choices: 1) you can decide to win, 2) you can decide to lose, or as one of my colleagues calls it, "Choose to Lose," or 3) you can let fate decide what will happen to you. Choice number two should be out of the question. Slackers choose this option, whether they do so knowingly or not. Having long since abandoned any thought they may have had in their lives about being successful, they see no way to win. They think that the deck's stacked against them, or that they've been treated unfairly, or they haven't been given the opportunity to succeed, or a whole host of other excuses that translate to one thing: "I'm comfortable with a losing mentality."

Coasters choose the third option. They usually see themselves as neither winners nor losers, but are often just adrift in the flotsam and jetsam of life. They wait for things to happen to them rather than choose to make things happen for themselves. My nephew, Dave, calls this the "Serendipity Theory of the Universe"—that one day, when you least expect it, the phone will ring with that new job offer, promotion, assignment or long-awaited contract. It's bad enough to plan your future waiting to win the lottery. It's even worse to plan on winning the lottery and wait in vain for someone to hand you a ticket. Clearly, that's not an effective strategy for an Achiever.

That leaves one option available to the success-minded individual: DECIDE TO WIN. Be purposeful, resolute and uncompromising in that belief. Failure should never be an option. Relying on fate is irrational. Given the alternatives, there isn't really any other choice.

> Paul needed a loan to expand his machine shop business after acquiring a new customer, who had given him what he said would be the first of many subsequent large orders for parts. Paul told me, "I sat there with the banker, petrified, with my hands shaking, knowing about the dangers and pitfalls of purchasing expensive equipment and hiring more operators while relying on only one customer to provide the income. I realized I'd be risking everything by relying only one customer to sustain my business, but I took the plunge and signed my name. As I prepared to sign the loan documents, I swallowed hard then forced my fear aside and made a decision to win."
>
> With that one decision, with that one simple action, Paul started on the road to wealth. His customer reordered even more complex parts with a higher dollar value, giving him more income and a higher return on his investment. The customer told other manufacturers about the high quality of Paul's work. With the additional machine tool capacity this business made possible, and with the additional operators he was able to hire, he had the ability to take on even more business.

Feel the Fear and Do It Anyway

Once you've made the decision to win, then you need to know whether you can handle fear. This is where it gets trickier because winning requires the ability to acknowledge fear, face it, feel it, touch it, and eventually let it go. As in our chapter on positive attitude, we've all heard so much on the topic. I believe that you must be able to handle fear as it can hold you in its grip—and a paralyzing grip it can be. It can hold you back from winning or from taking advantage of an opportunity. Fear of failure, of making a mistake, of what people might think, of speaking in public, of losing money, of rejection, and yes, even fear of success! You might come up with so many reasons for not doing something that you'll paralyze yourself and end up doing nothing at all. "I tried that before, and it didn't work," "Look at what happened to so and so," "I'm no good at that," "I can't stand rejection," "I don't have the time to do that right now," and, "She has more credentials than I do" are all excuses that keep you from deciding to win.

Making excuses is a cousin to another popular self-defeating thought process—the "What if ..." trap. This is a truly negative activity, as starting down the "What if ..." path simply creates undue anxiety in your life. You know the questions: "What if I can't do the job after all?" "What if this business I started fails and I'm up to my neck in debt?" "What if selling the new product line is harder than selling the old one?" "What if I tell the company how wrong they were about their decision, and they fire me?" "What if the joint venture I'm approving turns out to be a failure?"

To combat these fears, you might even make a little "game" out of it. Whenever you think of not taking action on a new idea or opportunity because of fear of failure, ask yourself this question: "What's the absolute worst thing that could happen to me?" Then, ask yourself a follow-up question: "Do I really believe this can happen to me?" More than likely, you'll answer your question with a "no."

Cheryl, the financial analyst, took a risk by accepting a demanding job in Colorado after the merger, and was told, "We only want 'stars' in our new organization." She's a great example of an Achiever who not only adapted to the merger and the new environment, but also decided to win. Here's what happened: When she saw all she had to give of herself to meet the job's demands, she asked herself, "What's the worst that can happen to me?

The worst might be that I'll gain experience and the wisdom of my experience will make me valuable to another company."

She decided to do her best and stay positive, but vowed that, regardless of the outcome, she would come out a winner.

Dan was one of my clients in a large manufacturing company. He was young, had energy and drive, and was the top sales producer. Even though he'd been with the company for only three years, they offered him the position of regional sales manager, passing over some who'd been there longer. It was a wonderful opportunity. Dan, though, felt quite secure and successful right where he was and believed he was destined to be in sales, not management. The thought of this new position and the increase in pay was exciting. He felt flattered, yet was intimidated by the responsibility. He said to me, "Look what happened to the last guy. He's out looking for a new job. I might end up with no job if I can't get the sales region to produce. Besides, I've never had any formal management training, and I don't have my master's degree. I'm not even sure I'd make a good leader. And what if I hate the travel involved?"

Dan and I went through the "what if's" and the "what's the worst that could happen" game. I told him, "Maybe the entire sales team will have no respect for you and laugh at you behind your back. Maybe by year-end, you'll have decreased sales by 100 percent and your name will be mud in the industry. Maybe you'll get fired and end up bagging groceries. Maybe you'll end up out on the street, broke and unhappy!" We looked at each other and I saw a faint smile come across his face.

Then I said, "Dan, you're the top sales producer in the company. Do you really think those things will happen to you? I don't think so! You're an Achiever, and you know it!"

Then I added, "By the way, Dan, don't think for one moment you won't be a fantastic regional sales manager. You're a winner with your customers and you have the respect and admiration of your colleagues. And everyone loves a winner. You already know what you need to do. Show your salespeople how you became the top sales producer and help each of them to become top producers. In your leadership role, make them feel they're working *with* you, not *for* you, and you'll be a huge success. Regarding your masters degree, remember that credentials are important, but character, determination, integrity, creativity, and drive count, as well."

Dan needed to make the decision to win. He was reluctant to see himself as anything other than a salesperson, for that was his "comfort zone." I can relate to how he felt. For many years I had made my living in the performing arts in concerts and industrial shows. I'd also gained a great deal of experience in the trade show arena creating and delivering presentations for companies such as IBM, NEC, Honda, Raytheon, Ray-O-Vac, Mazak, Con-Agra, Black and Decker, KomatsuDresser and numerous others. I enjoyed the excitement of the competitive environment where so many companies all vied for the attention of potential customers. Working with many organizations in a wide variety of industries had given me valuable insight into management and sales styles, as well as what makes for an effective corporate culture. It had also taught me about our volatile marketplace and its ever-changing inhabitants. I learned what works and what doesn't.

Eventually I considered starting my own company, offering programs on how to effectively sell, service, and manage people to gain a competitive advantage. I thought perhaps I might even incorporate my musical talent and offer truly unique programs. Could it work for me?

Then, one of my clients, Jim, a national sales manager for one of the largest distributors in the machine tool industry, asked me to participate in their annual meeting and help teach their technical people how to deliver a professional presentation. Customers were changing the way they made decisions to purchase high dollar capital equipment, and he realized that his technical people needed to help his sales force sell, but they lacked presentation skills. I seized the opportunity. I gave the seminar at the company's national sales meeting, and it was enthusiastically received. That gave me the courage to move forward. I decided to start my own company offering programs to help people and organizations beat the competition.

Was I scared I might fall on my face? You bet. I called my closest friends, Gayle Olson and Barbara Friedman, who, like the great friends they were, had always been my champions. We got together and went through the "what if's and what's the worst than can happen" game. It started with getting rejected, moved to audiences throwing tomatoes whenever I gave a presentation, and ended up in a scenario where I lost all my money in the speaking business and

became a bag lady pushing a shopping cart containing all my belongings. We laughed when we realized the absurdity of it all. They
encouraged me to move forward, and made me believe that my hard
work and initiative would never let that happen. My fear subsided.

Then, I made the decision to win. I developed new keynote
speeches and seminars, approached the clients I'd already won in
my trade show business, and forged ahead into this new venture,
picking up additional clients along the way. It took three years before I knew I would make it ... and it wasn't easy. Gayle and Barbara, and also Bob and Dotti Hovan, gave me an enormous amount
of support for which I'll be eternally grateful. Today, I feel fortunate that I made the decision to win, and when I look back at that
"what's the worst that can happen" conversation with Gayle and
Barbara, I smile and feel a great sense of accomplishment.

By the way, Dan, our reluctant sales producer, made the decision
to win, too. Today, he is no longer a regional sales manager, but a
successful national sales manager. He has the respect of the company's
entire sales force and has increased sales dramatically. He now gives
pep talks to his people on making the decision to win. He has a great
sense of accomplishment and doesn't know why he ever doubted himself in the first place. Give yourself permission to win, believe in
yourself and separate excuses from legitimate concerns.

Mike, a meeting planner for a telecommunications company,
recently told me, "Christine, I've lost my passion for booking hotel space, arranging travel, ordering food, hiring speakers, arranging audio-visual, and all the detail work involved in planning large
corporate meetings. What I really love is writing. I'm always asked
to write the humorous sketches for our yearly kickoff meetings
and I enjoy writing the witty speeches for employee anniversaries,
retirements and things like that. I've even written murder myster-
ies for fundraisers. I'd love to write those kinds of things for a
living because I can use my creativity."

"Then why don't you?" I asked. "What's the worst that can
happen?"

"People might think I'm not that funny. Besides, I have to be
realistic. It takes time to build up a new business, and I have three
kids! My wife wishes to stay at home to raise them, so I'm the sole
breadwinner for our family. I don't really have much money saved

so if I was to start a business and fail, losing my home would be a very real possibility. I can't give up my family's future to chase a dream."

"Mike," I said, "first of all, thinking you might not be funny is just an excuse. You have plenty of evidence to show that you can be successful in corporate humor. As for your income concerns, you may be right about the time it takes to develop a new business, but give yourself permission to win. Your fear is keeping you from seeing that you have more options than you realize. For instance, if you're willing to work hard, you can keep your job and develop your own business on the side. As you achieve success in your new venture and maintaining both jobs gets difficult, you'll come to a crossroads. If that happens, you'll have to make a decision about which road you want to take. But if you never start the journey, you'll never know which road you would have taken."

I'd like to say Mike took my advice, but the truth is, I hadn't told him anything that he hadn't already known deep down himself. He just needed confirmation that he could do it, and now, he is moving forward. Many people are waiting for someone else to give them permission to act when they themselves are empowered to do so. So will you decide to play it safe ... or will you decide to win?

Chapter 5

Avoid the Comparison Trap

When I decided to become a professional speaker, I picked the brains of as many successful speakers as I could without imposing too much on their time. Most were more than willing to give me advice and share their business strategies. I also sought counsel from the most successful entrepreneurs, executives, and managers I knew. I wanted to make sure that I learned from the very best. How did that sales manager from my trade show business motivate her people to increase their telecommunications equipment sales by 30 percent? How had that entrepreneur who founded an alternative fuel company managed to come out ahead of some of the more traditional power companies? How had my childhood neighbor become one of the key partners at Arthur Andersen with over 28,000 people reporting to him? How did my schoolmate become vice president of Sales for a Fortune 100 company? How did my real estate agent become a top producer? I was like a sponge, soaking it all in.

Also, I knew I needed to take stock of myself and examine my own personal traits. I concentrated on capitalizing upon whatever skills I had so that I could put them to work for me. I also looked hard and deep as to where I needed improvement. Then, I endeavored to acquire those skills. Over time, I learned that I needed to develop my own style, "walk my own path," and pursue my goals in a way that would work for me. I went through some real trials and errors, ups and downs, and made many mistakes before I could move forward.

Open Your Eyes and See

If you want to be at the top of your profession, I recommend that you seek advice. Listen and learn from those who excel in your chosen field. Put your own antennae out and study the Achievers who are getting the big sales, the promotions, large contracts and higher customer retention rates. Gather all the business intelligence, techniques and strategies you can from them, then consider these:

- What attitudes do they bring to their jobs each day? Do they come into the office saying, "Today, I'll make five new customer contacts"? Do they learn from recent failures, while refusing to dwell upon them? Successful people in any field put as much positive energy into their work as possible.
- What effective work habits do they have? Do they keep their work organized? Do they follow up quickly on leads? Do they pay attention to the details? They take every aspect of business seriously and find ways to improve their customers' businesses.
- What level of confidence do they portray when communicating with others? Do they display an air of conviction and ability? Do they sound authoritative without sounding authoritarian? Those who are successful not only possess the technical skills but can also communicate their ideas to others. You'll learn how in Section 3.
- What do they do when they listen to others? Do they ask questions? Are they as concerned with the ideas of others as they are with their own? Are they always trying to learn, even if they may be the most knowledgeable person around? Achievers understand that communication is two-way, and that we have two ears and one mouth for a reason.
- What levels of initiative do they show? Do they contact customers before customers contact them? Do they go to the boss with new ideas? Do they act on their instincts instead of waiting to be told?
- What goals have they set for themselves? Do they know what they want to accomplish before they begin a new initiative? Do they have goals for the year, the quarter, the month, and even the day? Success is not an accident; it's planned and purposeful.

- What do they do to enable others around them? Are they willing to share their knowledge with their peers and subordinates? Do they coach and encourage people to put forth their own best efforts? Those at the top are willing to help others find their way to the summit, as well.

When you ask yourself these questions, you'll realize that what sets successful people apart from the rest is more than just technical expertise—lots of people are technically competent—but Achievers bring to the table attitude, initiative, and much of the knowledge and skills we address in this book.

Here's where the "comparison trap" comes in. I studied the most successful professionals in my business and others, and made every effort to emulate them. I soon realized that all during the time I was seeking advice, I was making one big misconception. I thought that, if I used the same strategies and techniques as my successful peers and focused on the ideas of other knowledgeable business people, then they would work for me, too, and shorten my path to success. I thought that made sense. I was mistaken.

The insights and ideas of others can enrich the landscape along the path. They may even help make your path a little easier to walk. But what I learned was that there are no real shortcuts. Look upon those you admire as your role models, but don't think they have a magic formula that will work for you. Your role models will show you what you need to do, but don't fall into the trap of believing that doing the same things will work for you. You may indeed be able to duplicate some of their techniques, but thinking you need to turn yourself into a clone is a disservice to your own abilities.

After one of my seminars, "Creating a High Performance Workplace Through the Midst of Change," a young man told me, "In six months, my father will be retiring, and I'll be taking over the company. My father is respected, well liked and admired by both employees and customers. Although I know the business inside out, I'm worried that I'll constantly have to prove to everyone that I can fill my father's shoes. I'm worried that people will compare me to my father and expect me to be exactly like him."

I advised him to anticipate all of this, and encouraged him to be his own man, make his own judgments and blaze his own trail. This reminds me of a colleague of mine, Steve, who works for a small consulting firm in the field of performance improvement. The entrepreneur who founded the company is considered by her peers to be one of the best and brightest in the field. Judy creates exceptional rapport with clients and possesses insights that cause others to say, "I never looked at it that way before, but it makes sense."

She is also an expert communicator and develops client solutions that bring about desirable changes in individual and organizational performance. (We're talking about a woman who once created an operational definition of "common sense.") Judy had an innate ability to take abstract ideas turn them into concrete business plans.

Steve and the other associates in the firm were continually as impressed with Judy as the clients were. They would get together over lunch and in so many words, ask themselves, "How can we be more like Judy?" It took them several months to realize they could never be like Judy ... and to accept that that was okay. In fact, Judy herself never expected them to be like her. She had wisely hired the associates into the company not only because of their individual expertise, but also because of their own individual styles. Their mistake was in thinking that they could develop relationships the same way that she did and that they could have the same insights and the same communication style as her. They all studied Judy enough to recognize her fine qualities, but eventually realized that they each had to learn how to develop rapport and build relationships with clients using their own approach.

Sting and Elton John are both wonderful singers, but do they sound alike? Do they approach a song the same way? Is one person's vocal technique better than the other's? Would it work for Sting if he tried to copy Elton's style? Bill Gates and Larry Ellison are both dynamic entrepreneurs, but do they have the same leadership styles? Do they share the same strategic plan? The answer to all of these questions is the same: "Of course not."

So even if you've been in the game for twenty years, study your mentors, role models, gurus, and others you admire. Once they show you what's possible, don't fall into the comparison trap. Instead, identify what you're doing right and what you may be doing wrong. See yourself as others see you and take an honest inventory of yourself. Where do you need improvement? Where do you excel?

Chapter 6

Apply Creative Thinking for Business Solutions

W hen I ask participants in my seminars what they would like to learn about creative thinking, these are the typical responses I hear:

"I can't seem to reel in potential customers. If I could only think more creatively, I could get my foot in the door more often."

"I've become stagnant in my job. I feel as if I'm just going through the motions. I'd like to know how to think more creatively so that I can get out of the same old rut I've been in for years."

"I face a variety of different problems in the course of the day. I'd like to be more creative when it comes to solving problems."

"My employees are tired of pizza parties and 'Atta-boys.' Why can't I think of anything more creative to motivate my employees?"

"My boss keeps telling us we must 'think outside the box' for new product development ideas. I'm sick of that phrase. I don't even know what it means."

"I've never considered myself to be a creative person. Is it possible to become one?"

When I ask people what type of individuals they think are creative, they usually reply, "Painters, sculptors, writers, movie directors," and so on. I explain to them that creative thinking is a skill that anyone can learn and master.

I think of creativity this way: When used in music, the results are art. When used in life, the results are accomplishment. When used in the business world, the results are innovation.

Creativity can thrive in all areas of business. Many think it's an exclusive club for the marketing, advertising, or communication fields. This is not so. Anyone can join the club. Whether you're a mailroom clerk, a CEO, or someone in between, creativity is all around you and available to you. Yes, even computer programmers, accountants, and other professionals who tend to be more "analytical" can learn to be imaginative and resourceful.

Consider these applications in seemingly ordinary situations:

- All competitors want more than their fair share of business, and are plotting ways to get it. Sales representatives need to be creative in order to keep their existing customers and get new ones. If they can increase their sales, it's saying either that the competition has been complacent or that their imagination is paying dividends—or both.

- An engineer is often thought of as a scientist, but the application of theory is extremely abstract. There are usually an infinite number of solutions to a problem. Every new design and application requires creativity.

- An executive of an innovative company involves all employees in self-directed work teams and expects them to come up with better ways to service the customer, improve productivity and provide solutions to problems.

- An Internet company adds an "Instant Message" feature on their web site to handle customer inquiries.

- A manager at a manufacturing firm treats office systems and procedures as a challenge to his ingenuity. He constantly strives to find a way to streamline them. When he does, it challenges the status quo and upsets a few people, but ultimately, he feels the organization needs a wake-up call. It tells the decision-makers that if the company can increase its productivity by simplifying procedures, perhaps they need to examine them more closely.

- In her efforts to differentiate her presentations from those of her competitors, a professional speaker uses her talent as a violinist in her programs as a tool to demonstrate how we must treat customers. She emphasizes that we must treat customers as if they were Stradivarius violins—precious, invaluable, to be cherished, and handled with extreme care. (Sorry folks. Couldn't resist slipping that in.)

Never underestimate the importance of creativity if you want to beat the competition. It's just as important as being an Achiever, maintaining a positive attitude, being flexible through change and making a decision to win. When you're creatively inspired, you can challenge yourself to rethink the common ways you may be approaching your work. Creative thinking can liberate you from the usual constraints of your job and help you see that you don't have to do things the way you've always done them.

In fact, one trait of highly creative professionals is that they're able to deny many of the assumptions held by the organization. When they challenge the status quo and people respond by saying, "But we've always done it the other way," you can see the power of creativity. Who said there's only one way to explain financial products to potential customers? Who said there's only one way to design a hotel reservation system? Or communicate with your coworkers or staff? Who said meetings must always be in the conference room? Eliminate the rules. Most importantly, creative thinking helps you inject a new level of enthusiasm for anything you do.

To survive in business today and in the future, you must constantly create new ideas for every aspect of business. You must constantly generate new ideas just to survive! Bill Gates did not anticipate the Internet—in fact, he had to scramble to catch up! We are experiencing an economy based on innovation. You can win big just by out-thinking the competition with creative ideas. My wish is that this chapter will provide you with an invaluable conviction that an ever-present creative source is available to you. It will hopefully help you find your inner creative source, and understand how and where you can apply creativity to get the results you want.

Creativity Is Imagination

Let's take a moment to clarify what the term "creativity" means. The *Oxford English Dictionary* defines creativity as: "showing imagination as well as skill." Importantly, both "imagination" and "skill" appear in the definition. To reduce "creativity" to "imagination" doesn't fully explain the word. You can contrive very imaginative ideas that have no practical application: You can plan to open a retail location in the anticipated International Space Station, you can design a cheaper automobile made of fiberboard, or you can put chocolate on pizza.

While these may be considered imaginative ideas, creativity is more. True creativity adds "skill" to the definition. You need knowledge and expertise to help you distinguish between unrealistic and realistic ideas. Creative thinking occurs when you immerse your mental energy and tap into your imagination to create new products, seek fresh solutions to problems, or come up with novel approaches to your work—the so-called "thinking outside the box."

For instance, opening a new retail location in a Space Station might seem impractical, but what other, more realistic ideas might you come up with when you allow yourself to think creatively? McDonald's restaurants might have not yet penetrated the outer space market, but the hamburger enterprise has moved into several creative non-traditional retail outlets such as Wal-Mart, train stations, gas stations and airports.

Creative thinking also takes place when you imagine something that no one has thought previously. Perhaps you see something ordinary and then make a connection that no one has ever seen before.

A scientist at 3M was once trying to create a new adhesive and ended up developing a glue that didn't really stick very well. It would have been easy to dismiss the discovery, but this scientist realized there could be a practical application for his new adhesive. When he first started telling people about his idea, no one understood what he was talking about. He had to launch his own campaign to get the project off the ground. Today, most of us wouldn't know what to do without Post-It® Notes. And some of us go too far. I've seen people who have them on their computers, their phones, in their cars, in the bathroom and who knows where else!

The wireless radio was around long before Marconi worked on it, but no one could get it to work. It was Marconi who figured out that the antenna is what would make the radio operate.

How about the Walkman radio? The engineers at Sony tried to create a small portable tape recorder but failed, and the project was shelved. Then Masaru Ibuka, honorary chairman of Sony, decided to try to redesign it differently. One of the company's engineers had developed lightweight portable headphones. Ibuka suggested combining the two and excluding the recorder feature. Voila! The Walkman radio! It ended up becoming Sony's leading selling electronic product. Ibuka had used creativity to push beyond, around and through the wall.

Creativity occurs when you think of something completely new, but it does not always demand absolute originality. For example, as a musician, I can play a three-centuries old violin composition note-for-note but still give it my own musical interpretation. In business, a sales manager can enhance a traditional cash bonus incentive program to motivate employees by adding "bonus points" redeemable for merchandise. An engineer may conceive a fresh application of a centuries-old theory from Archimedes.

Anytime you rearrange information into a new order, or use old information in a new way, you're using your imagination. Albert Einstein said, "Imagination is more important than knowledge." In music, for example, it's safe to say there are only so many musical notes the ear can hear, yet people have been composing songs for centuries. When a songwriter sets out to write a new song, he knows he still might be able to create the most beautiful song ever written. He knows the notes are already there for him and he just has to put them together the right way to make the music memorable. Likewise, in business, the challenge can be the same—to organize familiar information in a fresh, new way. Think about it. You have probably collected a lot of customer data, but have you considered how the information you already have might lead to new sales? For instance, an insurance agent collects information on all of a customer's family members, but has she thought of marketing automobile insurance to dependent children when they reach driving age?

Consider these creative ideas:
- Scottish bacteriologist Alexander Fleming wondered why the lab's Petri dishes of bacteria failed to grow whenever they were left unwashed overnight near the open window. He soon realized the bacterial growth was slowed from the mold that blew in through the damp air. Penicillin was the result.
- When housewives kept slamming the door in David McConnell's face as he tried to sell books door-to-door, he decided to offer them a gift to prevent it from happening. He gave a small vial of his own homemade perfume. The women loved the fragrance so much that he quit selling books and founded Avon.

- Edwin Cox tried selling cookware door-to-door, but sales were poor because customers had a difficult time cleaning the aluminum pans. While seeking the best method to clean them, he learned that a little steel wool and soap gave him the best results. He made these soap pads and gave them away for free. Eventually, he threw away the pans and became a huge success with SOS.

- Richard Thieme (www.thiemeworks.com) speaks and writes about life on the edge, especially the impact of technology on life and work. He recalls a breakthrough that illustrates how creativity will happen if we are willing to keep ourselves on the edge and expect it. Back when the Internet was just coming into public awareness as a new medium, Thieme wrote an article for *Wired* magazine called "In Search of the Grail." Drawing on his 16 years as an Episcopal priest, he described how the new media might transform religious experience and organizations. He saw that the way we think about things and picture possibilities for ourselves are strongly influenced by the medium that brings those ideas and images to us.

  Wired liked the article and published it—but only after removing 90 percent of the 5,000 words he had written. Those words still belonged to Thieme, but what in the world could he do with them? He remembers sitting in front of his computer looking at the text of the article and the e-mail from the *Wired* editor, thinking, "What other magazines might be interested in articles about the impact of the Internet?"

  Now, Thieme had published his first short story—a science fiction story about a virtual reality machine back in the sixties. Like many freelance writers, he had learned to define the publishing world by reading *Writer's Market,* the bible of the marketplace that listed thousands of magazines. But *Writers Market* was a print book about print technology. Thieme never noticed that the horizons of possibility the book defined for him were in the United States. Every viable market in it was American! Because he saw no other options, he thought those markets were the only medium of print. Sitting in front of his computer staring at those 4,500 words, he had a revelation. The markets he could imagine had been determined by the world of print publishing. "Where can I send an article about the Internet?" He morphed the question into a different one: "How can I use the Internet to reach other markets?"

He began clicking through links—search engines barely existed then—and located magazines in other countries that were exploring the networked world. He located one in England, sent them a proposal for an article, agreed to terms, and had the article sent to them via e-mail within a week. A month later he was receiving e-mail from readers in Europe and has never looked back. Now his column, "Islands in the Clickstream," is read in countries all over the world.

That insight came because he was willing to engage the new technology and follow wherever it might lead. He couldn't see in advance from within the old model of reality what new horizons might open. We rarely see new possibilities from inside the old framework. That framework must go through a moment of transformation, a looking glass, an alchemical change from lead to gold, and that only happens when we put ourselves on the edge and are willing to explore, not knowing what will come.

That "not knowing" place is a precondition of creativity. Even though he was writing about the Internet, Thieme had not seen that the Internet itself determined that his market had become worldwide. Information was now easily available from other countries. The Internet created the means for delivering intellectual property and generated a worldwide audience.

Creative insight happens when we least expect it. But when we look back, we usually see that we allowed ourselves to think the unthinkable and that, says Richard Thieme, ripens the mind for new possibilities.

Can I Be Creative, Too?

Psychological studies have proven some people are, by their nature, simply more creative than others. Actually, scientific research about the difference between "right-brain" and "left-brain" people has shown that some people are more inclined to be creative than others. Dozens of books describe how the "right-brain" people of this world tend to be more action-oriented and think in terms of pictures. They have great vision and insight, and use their intuition to solve problems. They learn more through free exploration than long verbal explanations. "Left brain" people are more inclined to be detail-oriented and analytical "fact-finders" who think logically and rationally. They approach work in a structured, orderly way.

Does that mean then that, if you're a left-brain person, you should dismiss your hopes of becoming more creative? Research has also shown that very few people are without the instinct to be creative and resourceful. That potential is in all of us.

A question, then, may be plaguing you. If you have a creative source within you, why doesn't it appear more often? Why are you not more consistently creative? The answer might be that your fear of appearing foolish, or negative personal judgment, inhibits your creative side. The key is to give yourself permission to be creative. Many people are afraid of letting their creative side emerge, but once you believe you can be creative, then you've taken that first step into opening yourself up to new possibilities.

Enhancing Your Creativity

Creative thinking occurs differently for each person, so there's no one-size-fits-all approach that will work for everyone. If you want more detailed information about creative techniques, I encourage you to explore the variety of books on the subject, but here are a few techniques you might find useful.

Concentrate

Creative ideas may come to you through sharply focused and steadily sustained concentration. My friend Dr. Dan Yovich teaches a course on creativity at Purdue University. "One method to get creative ideas," he explains, "is to rub a pencil against paper while focusing on the situation or problem and the desired outcome. Steadily focused and repetitious activity such as this is a means for many people to channel into their subconscious where a variety of solutions and ideas will generally present themselves. Others simply stare into space with a far-away look in their eyes."

Reflect

Silent reflection is another method. Some people simply sit in a comfortable chair in a quiet room, keeping their mind open for whatever new ideas enter. Others sit in the park or drive up to the mountains to look over a peak, and jot down any idea that inspires them. Still others have told me they get their most creative ideas upon awakening from a good night's sleep. Their technique is to prolong the calm and peace of sleep for a few minutes before rising. In that serenity, ideas come more freely. Often, dreams provide us with messages we don't experience in state of awake.

Establish Rituals

Creative thinking takes place for many people when they're engaged in some type of ritual that helps keep their mind focused. Andrew Carnegie, for example, carried a deck of cards and played solitaire to clear his mind when he sought creative solutions to problems. Albert Einstein said he always got his best ideas in the morning while shaving! Many people, myself included, make a ritual of sipping their morning coffee in solitude and get their most creative ideas at that time.

Meditate

Meditation is not only what I call a "stress-buster," but when practiced correctly, it also calms the incessant stream of thoughts that sometimes flows through your mind like a raging river, bringing you inner quiet—a great place to seek creativity. You may think this is only for those who, like myself, practice yoga. If you do, you're very wrong.

Bob Hovan, a successful sales professional, is one of the most happy-go-lucky and funny people I know—and one of the most creative. He told me many years ago that whenever he needs to find a solution to a problem, make an important decision, or come up with something creative to win over a customer, he meditates anywhere from five to fifteen minutes. Because of his upbeat personality, I was surprised to learn he practiced meditation. He explained that solutions and ideas don't necessarily pop in his head during his meditative state but usually come to him soon afterwards. I know many business professionals who've said that meditation calms their minds while, at the same time, jolting their creativity.

The process of meditation does not happen by itself. It requires effort on your part. If you'd like to try it, begin by sitting or lying down in a quiet place. Be sure to keep your spine straight so that your energy will flow. Eliminate all the "to-do's" and "I gotta's" from your mind and concentrate on the inhalation and exhalation of your breath. Breathe deeply from your diaphragm. To be sure you are breathing correctly, place your hand slightly above your waist to feel the rise and fall of your lower chest. Then, listen to your breathing and your heartbeat. Shut out the rest of the world, and trust that all is well in your life and in the universe for those moments. If any thoughts interrupt your mind, push them out. Relax and let go.

Beginners, do this for five minutes. Getting to fifteen is excellent for a beginner. When possible, practice it up to a half an hour each day. You dozed off? That's good! You succeeded in putting yourself into a relaxed state and gave your mind and body a great way to rejuvenate, energize and receive ideas that may be skulking in some remote brain cavern. (Just be sure you don't do this at your desk unless you're self-employed!)

Huff and Puff

Most of those I work with tell me they get creative breakthroughs while enjoying recreational activities. I enjoy fast walking, bicycling, hiking, yoga, weight training, and gardening, and find that when I'm doing something I enjoy, I become completely oblivious to my work. This is when my subconscious mind releases my own creative imagination and ideas seem to pop into my head, which is why I always keep a pencil and paper nearby.

My colleague Cyndi Maxey, who heads up her own training and development company, once told me her most creative approaches to training are inspired in the shower or while exercising. Once while jogging, she created what she calls "the Oreo approach to warm-ups"—a three part system for trainers to follow when conducting a session warm-up activity. Trainers who use the Oreo Approach warm up the audience in three ways: to the trainer, to the topic, and to each other. Like the design of the Oreo, if one part is missing, it just doesn't "taste" the same. She persuaded RJ Nabisco to grant her permission to use the Oreo name. She even passes out Oreo cookies to help visualize and taste the concept. She has since had four articles published on this idea. All of this, she says, resulted from a kernel of an idea that hit as she was jogging.

When I ask my audiences where and when they get their best creative ideas, the following are the most common responses: talking with colleagues or friends, walking the dog, showering in the morning, in the middle of the night, on a plane, listening to classical music or during any type of exercise. Why these kinds of activities? Could it be because people feel a sense of balance, rhythm, harmony, mental relaxation, and healing in their life while engaging in them?

An executive in one of my seminars shared this: "When I get stuck in rush hour traffic, I've learned not to get myself into a tither because I know there's nothing I can do about it. To avoid frustration, I turn on my favorite Kenny G CD because it has a relaxing effect on me. That's when I get my best ideas."

He's on to something. Listening to Mozart or other classical music has been proven to enhance creativity and has helped many a college student cram for final exams. Ongoing studies are being conducted to determine the effect that music can have on the creative mind. Art Fry came up with the idea for Post-It® Notes during church choir practice!

Break the Rules

Creative thinkers are often those who are willing to throw away the "rule book." Innovation has occurred in every industry when a creative thinker questioned the status quo. Here are a few examples:

- Fred Smith broke the rule that only the U.S. Post Office could deliver mail when he founded Federal Express.
- In 1971, Starbucks broke the rule that an establishment that only served coffee could be successful by providing what many people today (especially this author) consider to be the "ultimate coffee experience." I consider Starbucks to be one of the most innovative companies in America today.
- Leo Burnett broke the advertising rule that words are more important than images when he achieved incredible success for clients with Tony the Tiger, the Jolly Green Giant,

the Pillsbury Doughboy, the Keebler Elves and my favorite, Morris the cat.

- Executives at all three major television networks predicted failure for Ted Turner's rule-breaking idea of an all-news station as three previous attempts of this format had failed. Today, even foreign dictators turn on CNN to learn what's happening in the world.

- Henry Ford received strong criticism in 1914 when he broke the rule that auto workers should be satisfied with the minimum wage of $2.34 a day and increased his workers' wages to $5.00 a day. Morale soared and productivity in the plant increased dramatically. Soon, his workers could afford to buy the cars they made! By 1916, the Ford Motor Company doubled its profits from $30 million to $60 million.

- Alfred P. Sloan, CEO of GM broke the rule that people had to pay in full for their car when it was purchased before they could drive it off the lot. He pioneered the idea of purchasing through installment payments.

Here's more food for thought on breaking the rules: how about eliminating some of the boring and unproductive meetings held in conference rooms where ideas get fogged up the moment the door is closed? Instead, take your people for a walk or have them sit on a staircase. I recall a client visit where I saw an example of this. As I pulled into the parking lot in front of their building, I saw a group of about twelve people sitting on the grass having a meeting led by a person who was obviously their manager. I sat in my car for a while just to observe. They were talking in the sunshine and open air where their minds could find fresh thoughts. He had them stand most of the time so their energy levels would be high. I found out later he often called these meetings spontaneously and did not allow phones, beepers or any distractions. What a creative manager!

Intuition Is In

Men call it a "gut feeling." Women call it "intuition." It's a type of thought process that comes from within us and offers a way to integrate and synthesize, as well as weigh and balance ideas and information. In the past, speaking about using intuition in business was considered frivolous. Today, the corporate world is taking the matter of intuition to heart. Many are training their executives to use intuition to help them achieve productive results.

Each of us has that strong little voice inside our head whose ideas we tend to dismiss as silly or irrelevant. Learn to trust your insights and remain open to divergent solutions. Believe that your intuition does exist and that it can be of use to you. Loosen any inhibitions you may have about it. Intuition may come out of nowhere and probably when you least expect it. Scientists and artists refer to it again and again in describing the key element in the act of discovery or creation. It's intuition at work. Don't muffle that voice, whether you hear it as a loud shout or a quiet whisper. If you have to make a big decision, hold off and wait until your gut tells you what to do.

Ideas for Success

Maybe our high school teachers were on to something when they forced us to keep a journal. Today, you can keep a daily journal and write down ideas, musings, pictures, or whatever else comes to mind. Keep it with you throughout the day so that you can capture ideas as soon as you think of them.

One of the most effective methods of keeping track of my ideas came from Jim Meisenheimer, a highly-successful sales trainer and author. I was fortunate enough to have Jim as a mentor in the early part of my speaking career. He told me to create an "Ideas for Success" journal and always keep it nearby—especially during a seminar. Whenever I get a creative idea, I write it in my journal then transfer it to the appropriate file in my "Ideas for Success" folder in my computer. Then I make sure I review them regularly. I even take this a step further. I take one idea at a time, implement, and practice it (just as when I had to practice fingering passages on the violin) until they become habit. That's how you can be more effective in implementing new ideas.

Because of all the daily "mind-traffic" we experience—all those things we need to remember to do, and responsibilities, both business and personal—sometimes we need to slow down in order to speed up. Countless business professionals have told me they need to stop what they're doing and write something down the moment they think of it or they'll quickly forget their great ideas. The alternative is to agonize over the forgotten great idea. Most people, myself included, do not want to admit this happens to them.

I recommend that you keep a running log of all the creative, innovative things you can think of. This will allow you to develop even your "half-baked" ideas into something that may be the spark of genius down the road.

Stretch Your Horizons

If you're an Achiever who focuses intently on your particular business, spend some time developing interests in other areas. Many times, a completely unrelated pursuit will serve as a source of ideas if you keep your mind open for unique connections and applications. Can reading about gardening designs give you fresh ideas for organizing a warehouse? Is there a connection between different fishing techniques and "landing" diverse types of customers? Can Civil War reenactments teach us about business strategy? Who knows? If you're open to divergent thinking, you might be surprised where new ideas come from.

One of my clients once got a great idea while scuba diving in the Caribbean. He decided to return later that year to take his sales force on a training experience that would stretch their horizons. He knew that many of the elite management training courses pit their people against the elements for several days for a team-building experience. In these basic survival courses, people have to work together and use their imagination in order to survive in the wilderness. He realized that scuba diving would be a unique twist on this idea because below the ocean waves, your field of vision is limited and you have absolutely no idea what might be around the next reef. You depend on a buddy and must use non-verbal communication to survive. He asked his sales force if they'd be willing to participate in this adventurous training event and they all responded with great enthusiasm.

While there, after giving the team several diving experiences, he took it even further. For those brave souls who were willing to participate in this exercise, he took them night diving on a reef. Night diving is very different from diving during the day because your field of vision is reduced to just the light beam you carry. Your focus must be intense, and you don't dare let go of your buddy.

He told participants to concentrate on letting go of fear and enjoying the serenity of the calm, warm water. (If I were on that trip, I would have had visions of *Jaws* and *The Perfect Storm!*)

The next day his team sat together and brainstormed ways to gain an edge over their competition. The ideas came quickly and, at the end of the day, they had a good strategy for moving forward. My client told me he believed the experience was successful because the scuba diving element had put everyone into a creative state while building a strong sense of camaraderie and team spirit. This manager spent a great deal of time and money to encourage creative ideas, but the rewards were well worth it. Sales increased 20 percent the following quarter and 15 percent the next.

Don't Kill Creativity

I've seen many managers inadvertently destroy creativity because of lack of time. This can actually hold back business growth, as today's workers need to stay creatively charged. One way to do this is to give the group a challenging problem to solve or come up with a new idea. As we will discuss in Section 2, this is an effective way to ignite the fire under some of the Slackers and Coasters. I recommend you provide them with specific goals but do not dictate how they should be met. They will use their own creativity if you permit them come up with solutions. You may wish to create a task force of people from different departments so that the diversity of talent and thinking styles stimulates discussion and energizes the group. You'd be surprised to see the strategic ideas these task force groups come up with.

Brainstorm

Most of us have participated in brainstorming sessions. If you haven't, you're missing an opportunity to discover how creative ideas can be introduced, developed, and expanded as thoughts are bounced from person to person. To effectively set up a brainstorming session, I recommend that you take people away from the office and bring them to a unique environment in order to foster their problem-solving skills. Identify the problems and generate solutions for each one. Then, ask, "Do we have an opportunity to do something that's never been done before and, therefore, will really differentiate us from the competition?"

Think Positively

Creativity requires a positive attitude! Think "Yes! I can find a better way to do this." Even if you receive negative feedback, it can provide the thrust for you to try a different approach.

Take It Easy

In today's world, we know we must work hard in order to succeed. But frankly, if you're overworked, developing creative solutions will be more difficult. Take a break from your problems and slow down a little. As I said earlier, often the best ideas present themselves when *outside* the work environment, as in the slogan: "You deserve a break today ...." Take one soon. In fact, take a vacation if you can. Doesn't that sound sweet?

Section 2 offers examples of how others have used creativity in their job, and ideas that will help you take a more creative approach to business. Remember that highly creative individuals are not necessarily members of Mensa, but they do march to the beat of their own drum. They do immerse themselves diligently into whatever they do, are willing to take risks and are open to new ways of looking at the world.

I encourage you to try some of the ideas in this chapter to tap into your own creativity. The more often you focus on innovation and insight, the more likely you are to develop unique ideas on a regular basis. Having a competitive edge means having a creative edge. And, having a competitive spirit is important. It leads to increased productivity and the best of creative new ideas. Wherever you are, open your mind and let your thoughts flow free.

Section 2

Be Smarter and More Creative than Your Competitors

Whether you're an entrepreneur who wants to beat the competition to a new product introduction, a sales professional who wants to get the order, or some other hard-working person who wants to get ahead in your job, here's a very simple observation and the main subject of this book: There's always another numbers wizard out there who also offers financial-planning services. There's always another go-getter out there who also sells communications equipment, or another guy out there who thinks he can manage employees better than you can. Even if you're fortunate enough to be the only player in a niche market today, someone else will discover your success and give you a run for your money. There's always someone trying to do what you're doing. What you need to keep in mind is this: To them, *you're* the competition and you should be setting the bar for them.

I consult with the owner of an event production company who wastes a lot of her energy griping about her competitor's success. She complains endlessly about the corporate clients she has lost to them. "They have more sales representatives, more working capital, and can offer more services than my company. How can I possibly compete?" She always feels one step behind and cannot seem to transcend her frustrations.

I keep telling her, "Stop obsessing about what your competitor is doing! Spend your energy thinking of innovative ways to differentiate your company from hers. Concentrate on developing strong relationships with your existing clients, provide exceptional service and focus on ways you can be better than them. You need to turn your complaints into questions: 'So what is it that makes them a more successful event production company than mine? Do they have better marketing? Can I offer a service they don't?' "

Instead of agonizing over her competition, she should be learning about them and from them as described in the next chapter.

Sales professionals complain to me about their competitors all the time. I hear them say how they tried to establish relationships with potential customers only to have a competitor woo them away. They dwell on the injustice. They shout "unfair" or "I was there first!"

To them I say, "So you caught a flight to Texas, delivered a flawless presentation, offered a competitive price, took the client for an expensive dinner, and you still lost the deal? Tough. This isn't the schoolyard and the playground monitor isn't going to make your competitor go to the back of the line. Now, what are you going to do about it? Who said life was fair? Accept this fact of life: Sometimes the dragon wins."

Never spend more than a few minutes bemoaning disappointments. You have more important business to attend to. Figure out why your competitor got the business and why you didn't. Improve your selling skills and be sure you're applying the techniques we discuss in the chapter for sales professionals. Apply what you've learned then move on. Trust that tomorrow you'll be the one to get the sale and the "other guy" will lose out.

Let's not forget to mention the "competition" that exists within our own companies. Like it or not, we're always judged against our colleagues, and the reality is we're not all going to get the promotions or choice assignments. The key difference between competing with your peers and an outside competitor is that you need to collaborate with your peers in order to accomplish the company's goals. I hear employees grumble that no matter how hard they work, they cannot advance in their jobs, or that someone else got promoted instead of them. Again, instead of harboring bitter feelings against your successful coworkers, you should first be happy for their achievements, and second, learn what you can from their successes.

Ask these questions: What did they do to advance in the company? Were they better than you at building customer relationships? Did they have a better understanding of the boss's expectations? Did they *ask* for the promotion? Did they offer solutions to problems, or better yet, handle them on their own? Do they possess skills you lack? Find out what made them successful, and then vow to do it better.

Cora is a mid-level manager in a Fortune 500 company. She was amazed that her colleague Barbara had been promoted to Regional Manager, making her Cora's new boss. "I don't get it," said Cora. "Barbara never had a deep understanding of the work our department does. Furthermore, she delegated everything to her subordinates so she could leave early every day. The other managers and I stayed late each evening working our tails off, yet she's the one who was most popular with the vice-presidents."

After discussing this with Cora, I helped her realize what Barbara does well is *communicate!* Barbara always informed her boss about the progress her group was making toward their goals, what new initiatives they had begun and, when appropriate, if important deadlines might be missed. When she could, she explained in advance what action her group would take to handle problems. While Barbara might not have been very popular with her coworkers, the bottom line is she gets results. I advised Cora to think about the extraordinary potential she would have if she could combine her excellent technical prowess with Barbara's ability to communicate.

Contrast Barbara with Ted who had the same position in the company as Barbara but managed another team. Both reported to the same boss. Ted had the technical expertise but never kept his boss informed about his group's progress like Barbara did. Ted should have realized that whether the boss asked him or not, he needed to be kept informed. When the end of the year arrived and he finally communicated that there might be some serious challenges ahead, the boss asked, "Why haven't you been discussing this with me all along?" Ted's group had worked just as hard as Barbara's, but his "don't ask, don't tell" policy did not score him any points. Rather, it put him on the other side of the door after the company's last Reduction in Force.

Ultimately, Cora realized holding on to bitter feelings about her boss wasn't going to get her anywhere. She realized she needed to take stock of her own shortcomings, and be sure never to make the same mistake Ted made. When Barbara gets her next promotion, Cora now believes she is next in line to replace her.

Whether you're an employee seeking a promotion, a sharp executive who would like to know how to win over employees when instituting change, a customer service rep who wants to know how to handle difficult customers or a salesperson who wants to be able to meet and achieve your goals, you must be smarter and more creative than your competitors. No matter where you're positioned in the enterprise, you need to look deeply inside yourself and your company to determine what type of culture, techniques and skills you need to assure a more successful future for yourself and your company. Then you need to take action fast. This section will help guide you there.

Chapter 7

Know Your Competition ... and Outshine Them

The competition is always closer than you think. Every company is ready to launch the next great product, get your customers and steal your talent. No one knows who or what may be waiting around the corner. One of your goals should be to help your company become the market leader. That includes knowing what your competitors are up to so you can determine how to maintain an advantage. This process requires you to obtain and process market intelligence and do so in measurable and comparable ways. In other words, compare apples with apples and know your competition cold.

In the past, conducting a competitive analysis was considered a daunting task as companies did everything possible to keep pricing and product development information a secret, and consultants were paid large fees to do them. Today, you don't have to be a James Bond or pay a high-priced consulting firm to keep an eye on your rivals. Thanks to the World Wide Web, you can learn more about the competition faster than ever. (In fact, the home page of the site www.WebsMostLinked.com actually encourages you to "spy" on your competitors.) Today's technology is one of the best means of gathering information about your competitors. (That's why you shouldn't put anything on your own web site you don't want *your* competitors to know!) The Internet offers a remarkably wide variety of sources—content-rich Web sites, news services and other competitive information.

Don't chase down every competitor and spend a great deal of money to do it either. It's simply not practical. By the time your survey and analysis is completed, your information may already be obsolete. Time is of the essence, so do it and be done with it. Then take what you learn and evaluate what you and your company need to do better. Be sure to keep this one thing in mind as you go about your analysis and every day thereafter: The competition exists only to make you *outshine* them. Doing a competitive analysis and reporting to your company is important, but it's never so important that you become preoccupied with it. If you do, it will hold you back from developing a sound strategy to beat them.

In large organizations, it's usually the job of the marketing department to perform a competitive analysis and report to their people. Recently, I delivered a sales training seminar where the marketing manager provided their sales staff with an amazingly thorough analysis of the company's two top competitors. She had so much information on them that the handout was an inch thick. It provided everyone with the knowledge we needed to determine how to beat them in our sales approach.

To perform an analysis of your competition, answer the questions and consider the comments in each area listed below. Some of its content may seem elementary for some readers but others may find that it will open their eyes to the importance of gathering information on the competition and making sure they surpass them in all areas.

Company Background Information

- **Who are your key competitors?**
  List them. The more competitors you have, the more critical it is to distinguish yourself in the marketplace. If your company is larger than your competitors, you may have many advantages over smaller competitors. If your competitors are larger than you are, then you may be able to take advantage of your smaller size and move more quickly in the marketplace. You may also be able to convince customers to buy by stressing that you can offer more personalized service and concentrated attention.

- **Where are they?**
  In an increasingly global and technology-oriented marketplace, your competitors may be located overseas, down the street, or of course, exist entirely on the Internet with no physical location. They may also be found in non-traditional businesses. For instance, banks are now offering insurance products whereas in the past this

was a market reserved for insurance companies. Telecommunications companies are providing Internet services and satellite TV is in direct competition with cable companies who in turn have added Internet services. Many placement agencies are providing training on hiring and retaining quality employees creating competition for training and development companies. Starbucks is selling desk-accessories. K-Mart, Wal-Mart and other discount retailers are fast becoming the largest retail grocers in the country. This holds true for small businesses as well. Beauty salons are now adding spas to their business. Accountants are offering financial investment services. Landscapers are now providing snow removal. Meeting planners are now offering complete service—travel arrangements, scripting, entertainment, stage production, audio-visual, conference gifts, and much more. Many businesses are increasingly moving toward becoming more full-service organizations. If you're a small business, it may be to your advantage to expand your offerings through vertical integration to be able to retain your current customers.

- **How many branches do they have?**

  If your competitor has branches that are congregated in a given geographic area, you may wish to move into market locations they may have overlooked. You can then advise potential customers that you can ship from an area closer to them and save them money on shipping costs. Also, your competitor's strongest profit center is probably close to their headquarters and may even be a cash cow. Perhaps other competitors have been reluctant to move near them, and you might consider setting up a branch in that location to give them a run for their money. You may even want to move into markets in another country. Many manufacturers headquartered in other countries obtain much higher prices in their area due to the lack of competition. This would be another opportunity to move in on their territory if you have a price advantage.

- **How many warehouses?**

  If they have an extensive warehouse and distribution network, it may be easier for them to provide products to customers quickly. At the same time, an extensive warehouse system can be more costly to operate in overhead inventory holdings and staffing levels.

- **What are their products and services?**

  Your competitors may offer a full product line or may focus on a few select products. The more you know about your competitor's products and services, the better you will be able to evaluate how your offerings differ from theirs and what new features or products you should develop.

- **What do they offer that directly competes with your business?**

  In what products or services do you compete with them head to head? If you're a banking organization, for example, there may be little difference in what you offer from your competitors. Every aspect of how a customer does business with your bank and the experience they have when they call, come in, or use your on-line services must be different and better. The level of service you give to customers after opening a commercial account must also be different and better. This holds true for any business where you must compete with them head to head.

Marketing and Advertising

- **How and where do they spend their marketing and advertising dollars?**

  In which magazines, trade publications, newspapers and journals do they advertise? This will give you an indication of the markets they're trying to reach. Your competitors may also advertise locally or nationally. Some advertise more during a given time of year. Some companies run constant promotions; some run a single ad. Keep in mind that repeated promotions generate more business and name recognition than a one-time ad.

- **How much would you estimate they spend?**

  If they begin spending more than usual, determine whether or not they're trying to aggressively build their customer base or desperately trying to regain market share. If they spend very little on advertising, why is that so? Could it be because they have strong word of mouth advertising and referral business? Or, could it be that they may be facing financial difficulties?

- **What products, features, and benefits are they advertising?**

What your competitors see as worthwhile can help your company be more selective in determining how to compete. And, how they market their products gives you an idea of the type of customer they're trying to attract. For example, Virginia Slims targets today's Superwoman. Total cereal is targeted to today's active health-minded individual. The Land Rover is targeted to the affluent suburban housewife. The size of your business doesn't matter in this area. A beauty salon in my neighborhood advertises transportation services. They obviously target elderly clients. RentaHusband's target market is obvious. Justballs is a unique Internet company that specializes in all types of athletic balls. You may need to decide if you wish to go after the same markets, focus your direction in a different area or specialize.

- **In which trade shows do they exhibit?**

If your company doesn't exhibit in a trade show where your competitor is exhibiting, there must be a reason they're there. Find out why. If you're exhibiting in the same industry shows, you must make every effort to differentiate your booth from your competitors' to ensure your product will be more memorable to customers. Never rely on show management to bring people to your booth. It's *your* job to bring buyers to your exhibit. This requires effective pre-show promotion with a sound marketing strategy. Without these, exhibiting in a trade show can be a waste of valuable time and money.

Find out if your competitor is hosting a special event in conjunction with their trade show. If they are, and have properly promoted it prior to the show, they'll have a better opportunity to get a group of customers in one room and have their undivided attention—away from YOU! In this case, you need to create that same type of opportunity and outshine them by sponsoring an event they won't want to miss. Just be sure it will be fun, is promoted properly and the cost is within your budget.

- **World Wide Web**

Look at your competitor's web site frequently. See if they're using it merely to provide information about their products and services or whether customers are able to place orders on their site. Estimate how much they invested in their site.

If you look at the complexity of the site's graphics, the amount of interactivity and the detail of its content, you can assume that they've made an important investment in their site and they take it seriously. Smaller businesses may have a presence on the web just because it's the popular thing to do, and never really take full advantage of the site's potential.

Is their site more impressive or functional than yours? How dynamic is the content, and does it give customers a reason to return to their site? Is it updated frequently so customers are apt to return? Do they often add new specials or new pages offering tips, advice, or industry information? Do they offer media content?

Are customers able to check inventory from their site? I've often heard customers of John Deere and Okuma state how they appreciate being able to interact with the company 24 hours a day, 7 days a week because it saves them time.

How fast do they respond to Internet inquiries? Order something yourself or send them a question. If they don't respond within a few hours, that may indicate service capacity issues with their website. Often I've had to wait three days for a response from major corporations when I've done this. If you can respond within four hours or less, you definitely have a competitive edge.

Distributor Relationships and Reps

- **Do they sell their products through distributors or reps?**

How is your competitor's product distribution structured? Some companies structure their reps by product line, while others structure their reps by product type or by location. Do the reps promote only one product line? Those who do might be more inclined to "hustle" more because they don't have another company's product to rely on or seasonal incentives to push a particular line. What kind of margins or price breaks do the reps enjoy? Is the line they rep considered highly desirable in your industry.

Do they feel the product they represent is not being marketed, advertised and serviced effectively? Does their product have a glitch that has caused frustration for them or their customers? If they're not confident in the company or product they represent, you may be able to win them over to become a distributor for your company. I've seen this occur many times throughout the years. One of my past clients is a software provider in a large industry. Its sales people complained to me about a glitch in one of their products that has caused big problems for many of their customers and has been an embarrassment to them and their trainers. One told me the company has had this glitch for so long that she's ready to call their biggest competitor.

Market Direction

- **Where are they headed?**

It's obviously important to know what direction your competitors are heading and what growth strategies they may have announced. You don't want to be surprised if they're planning to penetrate new markets or begin an aggressive growth campaign. Knowing this will help you shape your own strategies. Pay attention to which products or services they're promoting heavily.

Where are they spending research dollars? Companies investing in product development take their future seriously. They position themselves to be long term players in the marketplace. Those who do not focus on innovation will soon be surpassed by competitors who do invest in their long-term viability.

Financial Information

- **How are your competitors performing financially?**

This information is readily available from Internet services: www.firstcall.com and other similar Internet companies that offer broker-oriented material on companies. Companysleuth.com is a foolproof way to make sure you know what your top competitors and customers are up to. Register at the site, list up to 10 public companies and they'll deliver daily e-mail briefings to you on analysts' ratings, stock trades, as well as patents. Knowx.com provides public records on bankruptcies and lawsuits. You can get the scoop on just about any person or firm named in a public document. Hoovers.com profiles more than 50,000 companies. You can also look up analyst reports, earnings estimates, and public records. Various business publications, Internet financial services, stock broker reports and, if they're a public company, their annual report all contain valuable data.

Seek and Ye Shall Find Key People

- ### Who are their key people?
  It's vitally important to know who the key people are in your competitors' organizations. I've often observed that market acceptance can be very closely related to who's running the ship. What is their background? How long have they been with the company?

- ### Who's steering the ship?
  Is your competitor's president or CEO well respected in your industry? Does he or she have a reputation for being a dictator? If so, this will likely lead to high turnover. I worked with one of the largest property development organizations in the country that had recently merged with another. The CEO of the new organization had a reputation for having a staunch bureaucratic management style. Many people who came from the company that merged with it were thrown off balance because of his bureaucratic style. The organization was in chaos for the first six months. In a situation such as this, you may be able to sway some of their people to come to work for you.

  Find out the president's leadership approach. Is he or she considered to be a conservative or radical thinker? Also, if a new officer comes on board, that may signal a change in the company's direction. Keep your eyes and ears open.

- ### Who are the "big wheels?"
  Again, check their web site to see if they have key personnel web pages. Dejanews.com is a search engine that tracks online discussion groups, and corptech.com provides information on 45,000 high tech companies and more than 170,000 executives.

  Attend conferences and see who your competitor has sent. Remember that companies usually send their best people to conferences. You can also acquire information from directories, trade-show books, the State Service Directory at your local library, from a headhunter, or simply by talking to people at industry association meetings and conferences. You can also purchase business directory software or simply use other Internet services such as on-line job postings and discussion groups. Just beware of the trail you leave behind!

Some Information *Is* More Difficult to Obtain

• Who's coming and who's going?

Good companies have positive cash flow, growth and profitability. Their executives are held responsible for business results. so if a company stagnates, regardless of the reasons, changes are necessary. The company goes on a diet, goes out and gets a bigger suit to allow it to grow again, or gets acquired. If you learn your competitor is losing an executive or manager, that just might be your chance to get their business or protect your own. If you can monitor your competition's key people, whatever information you can obtain may signal an opportunity for you to take action. You may need to use a little creativity to learn this information. Sometimes you can find a key employee's resume posted on the Web. Some of it might be obtained from your customers or other suppliers. However, if you ask them about your competition, be sure to be discrete. Also realize that some of the information you receive may be based on rumor.

• Gather group intelligence

A mistake many companies make is sending people to trade shows and not reminding them to walk down the aisles and check out the competition, and to attend networking events separately. Be sure to remind them to do so and take careful notes. Tell them to huddle afterwards to pool what they learned. Remind them not to forget to find out who may be coming in and who may be going out.

• What do job applicants say?

One of the best sources of acquiring the inside story about your competitors can come from disgruntled former or current employees who are looking for a job at your company. Be sure to remind the job interviewers in your company to tactfully ask questions and draw answers from job candidates when they interview.

One of my clients got the inside scoop on their biggest competitor in this way. This candidate was not only unhappy with the culture of her company, but she had also been passed over for a promotion. She was happy to spill the beans about other key people in the company who were also unhappy, and even mentioned that her employer just lost their biggest client. My client moved fast to solicit the client her company lost and offer jobs to the people she mentioned who were also dissatisfied. Within the next three months, two of the top people in her company left their jobs and went to work for my client.

- **What's good for the goose ...**

  Now we get to the hardest part and the main reason for performing an analysis. Once you have completed an analysis of your competitor, ask yourself those same questions about your company. Take a hard look at the business from the perspective of an outsider. In other words, "step out to look in." Imagine that you're one of your competitors or customers and go through the following.

- **How do your customers and competitors see your company's operation?**

  Their perceptions may be radically different from your own. What you may perceive as a well run, efficient company may not be the same perception your customers have formed. This, of course, is why it's so important to *ask* and *listen* to customers to get their feedback.

- **What's the reputation of your company?**

  Remember that today's customers are more likely to give their business to a company that has an outstanding reputation. Organizations such as Rubbermaid, Home Depot, GE, Nordstrom, Earthlink/Mindspring and Midwest Express Airlines all have a reputation for standing behind their products/service and providing outstanding customer service. How's yours? If you've had bad publicity regarding, say, a major product recall, an environmental or health violation or a discrimination lawsuit, turning the reputation around will be an enormous task. Every company says they have a good reputation but that's not necessarily true and customers can easily learn about your quality rating on the Internet. So, give yourself an honest assessment of what your reputation really is. And can you back it up with customer testimonials and customer satisfaction surveys?

- **What's your company doing to ensure a successful future?**

  All too often corporations get fat, sloppy and complacent about their products and services. Then along comes a competitor who's been lurking in the reef below with a "knock-off" product and the company has to scramble. Over the years, I've seen this occur again and again, in every trade show, in every industry. No sooner does a company exhibit a prototype of some new product or advertise an upgraded version of an existing product or service then, within a few months, the "knock-off" shows up from one of their competitors. You may remember that in the early 1980s, the Cabbage Patch Kids dolls were the hottest selling toys on the market. After Coleco had introduced this line of dolls and achieved great success with it, they became complacent and didn't introduce any new toys to the market. They thought the music would keep on playing with the same song. As a result, they went bankrupt in 1988. Only recently have Cabbage Patch dolls come back on the market, but the label now reads the name of another company.

  One of my trade show clients produced a new type of electric heater. This "first-of-its-type" product used a ceramic material for its heat source. The heater was cleaner, safer and more efficient than any electric room heater previously sold. For two years this new company made a real killing on the product and was able to sell it at a high price because it was unique to the marketplace. Within eighteen months, the knock-offs appeared at much lower prices. The party was over. Both Coleco and this company are strong examples of why no organization can ever get too comfortable even if they have a hot item.

  The speed with which your competitors can copy even the best ideas is increasing, which means that the time interval is decreasing between you coming up with a new idea and introducing it to the marketplace and a competitor showing up with a similar product. It's happening in all industries—both in products and services.

  In the case of a service organization, a competitor may have come up with a new twist to providing a similar service. Peapod.com no sooner began to offer its services before they had fierce competition from Webvan.com.

  Think of the insurance industry. Almost everyone who needs insurance has what he or she needs, so the best way to secure new customers is to take them away from your competitors. Traditionally, insurance was sold through either exclusive or independent agents. Several upstart insurance companies figured out a new way to sell their products. Instead of distributing through an agent force, these companies began selling insurance through 800 numbers and Internet web sites. Now, the staid insurance industry giants are scrambling to keep pace with these newer entrants.

Again, in which areas does your competition appear to have an advantage and where does your company excel? How does your website measure up to theirs? Remember that your website speaks about you to everyone in cyberspace. It relates who you are, what you do and don't do, and how well you do it. Be sure your cyber presence speaks well of you.

If this method of analysis appears to be too complex, perform a simple strategic analysis such as that suggested by Kenichi Ohmae, managing director of McKinsey Consulting of Japan, in his classic book, *The Mind of the Strategist.* It involves three C's:

- *Customers:* Divide your customers into as many categories or groups as possible (age, lifestyle, frequency of purchase, size order, gender, residence or company location, income, etc.). Then look at each group as a niche in terms of its specific needs and how they're being satisfied. Next, look at the needs that are not being satisfied adequately and how they might be improved.
- *Competitors:* Rank your key competitors in terms of how well or poorly they satisfy those needs.
- *Company:* Rank your own company in the same terms and analyze how it might best satisfy the unmet needs of the specific groups of customers. Where there's a good fit between your company's strengths and the gap left by the competition in satisfying the unmet needs, then that's where there may be an opportunity to design a "knock-your-socks-off" offering for that special group.

Wake Up Your Company

After you've completed the analysis, determine whether your company is headed in the right direction. If you feel it's not, or your organization is missing the boat in marketing, advertising, training, services, or any of the above, you need to honestly inform your decision-makers and not become intimidated by communicating the truth.

You may feel that it's not your responsibility to do this, but if you care about the success of your organization and your livelihood, then you have nothing to lose by displaying the evidence. Perhaps a truthful, factual report will shake things up with the powers that be. I wouldn't hesitate to bring your information and opinions to the table. Certainly, this information is key to your company's survival and your job security. Hopefully your company will take the right action.

Set the Bar

I'm sure most of us would sleep better at night if we knew we had no competition out there. We wouldn't have to rush new products to market, and could sell at our own pace. We wouldn't have to spend a great deal of money on advertising, and could set our prices however we wanted. Sounds great, doesn't it? Well, business isn't that simple.

Just try to get a good night's sleep and remember this: despite all I've said about the importance of knowing your competition, you should never become obsessed with them. Remember that your competitors are there only to challenge you to perform better. Your company needs to set the bar for your competition. In other words, be proactive, not reactive. Under no circumstances should the competition dictate how you compete in the marketplace because if it does, you'll simply be copying them and will never be out in front. A competitive analysis and report to your company is important because knowledge is power.

The competition is everywhere. Our entire economy is based on competition. Decide where you want to be in the marketplace. Will you be at the top, the middle, or the bottom? If you want to be at the top you must do your best to outshine them.

Chapter 8

Listen to Customers and Learn

Today's customers have higher expectations, more choices, and are more cost-conscious than ever. I believe that perhaps the biggest difference in the way we do business today and how we'll do business in the future is that we'll all have to be better at listening.

It's important for everyone in your company to put their ears to the ground and *listen* to what customers have to say. I'm not referring to conducting market research or checking out the competition on the Web. Even though these are wise business activities, I'm talking about *really listening*.

It is well-known that the cost of searching for new business is higher than the cost of retaining existing customers. If you listen to what your customers are saying, they'll tell you what you need to do to keep their business. Listening will also provide you with what product enhancements you may need and what problems may exist in manufacturing or service.

This chapter is for everyone in your company. Whether you're in sales (there's important information on listening applicable to sales professionals in the next chapter), are a customer service rep, an accountant, an executive, a credit manager, research and development specialist, an administrative assistant, a warehouse manager, or a technician, it's your job to uncover customers' needs and report them quickly.

Why Don't You ...?

Have you ever wondered why the airlines (why is the airline industry such an easy target?) don't warn you that there'll be no real food served on the plane? Sure, your ticket had "Snack" printed on it, but you held on to the blind hope that you'd receive something more substantial than those stale pretzels or salty peanuts that cause you to retain water during the flight and make you even more uncomfortable. Worse yet, your flight is early in the morning, and now your breakfast consists of coffee and peanuts on an empty stomach. You turn to vent to the poor flight attendant, who you know doesn't make the rules, and say, "I paid $600 for my ticket. WHY DON'T YOU serve something more?" The flight attendant smiles, gives you a feeble answer, and hands you another packet of peanuts.

Of course, you know that your ticket price includes more than the cost of your "snack." Since the captain has yet to inform the passengers that they can begin using their electronic devices, you can't help doing the math in your head: 15 peanuts at $600 a ticket comes to $40 a peanut.

Something else that irks me is: Why don't they hire competent baggage handlers? Why do they send your bags to Alaska when you're going to Texas? And, when passengers check their baggage with them, the law states they must ask, "Has anyone unknown to you asked you to carry any item for them in your suitcase?" (How would you even know about it if the person was unknown to you?) And, "Have your bags been in your possession since you packed them?" Think about it, if you'd checked your bags at your hotel and the bellhop had put something in it, how would you know? And certainly you wouldn't tell that to the agent because they might call security.

Another one of my biggest gripes: Have you ever had the experience of calling your credit card company's 800 number expecting to find a live person to help you? You get ten options but oddly enough rarely do you hear: "If you'd like to speak to a customer representative ..." So you try to find a different 800 number to see if there might be a live person there and you spend so much time trying to find a real person that you finally just give up in frustration. Then incredibly, you get a telemarketing phone call from your credit card company trying to cross-sell insurance. Finally, a live person! You say, "WHY DON'T YOU tell your people I need a phone number to speak to a live person about my account." She tells you, "That's not my department," and gives you the 800 number you called the first time. (This actually happened to me.)

How about these: WHY DON'T YOU delight customers with live instant messaging so customers can ask your service reps real-time questions through a pop-up window? (Check out *bikeshop.com*)

WHY DON'T YOU include batteries in the packages of kid's toys and electronics? WHY DON'T YOU make more lemon pies on Saturdays when you always seem to run out before 3:00 p.m. every week? WHY DON'T YOU have a web site that's easier to navigate? WHY DON'T YOU have a phone system that offers callers an option to press "0" for the operator when someone calls your direct line? WHY DON'T YOU sell printer cartridges that are refillable? WHY DON'T YOU give instant rebates at the cash register instead of troubling busy people to fill out forms, attach receipts, place them in envelopes and mail them before being able to get their rebate?

Anytime you or someone in your company hears a customer ask, "WHY DON'T YOU ...?" learn to recognize it as a strong signal that you need to *listen* to the customer, then respond to a service problem, product enhancement, or whatever additional service the customer is seeking.

"Why don't you ...?" has several cousins for whom you need to listen attentively. You may also hear "I think it would be great if you could ...," "Have you ever thought about ...?" or, "I hate to trouble you, but ...."

"Why don't you ...?" has many relatives, and the easiest way to recognize them all is to learn to listen anytime where a customer offers a suggestion or indicates a problem exists, such as:

- "Why don't you offer after-hours service?"
- "Do you offer a model that fits inside a smaller space?"
- "I don't know if I can operate the panel. It's not labeled very well."
- "I hate to be a pest, but the case broke again. Could I have another one?"
- "It would be great if you could have a technician on site.

Anyone might hear statements like these but whenever they're directed to you, you must respond by informing the company.

Whether your company provides a product or service, you must know your customer's business well and see it as your responsibility to make sure customers understand what you provide. But your tendency may be that you see communication as being one way: "I'll tell them what my business offers and they'll listen." In today's consumer market the true winners are those who recognize that customers are a valuable source of input for improving products and services as well as a source for new ideas. If your customers are politely offering a suggestion, and especially if they're complaining about something, consider yourself lucky when they tell you how they feel. Most of the time, customers won't even bother to let you know if they have a problem. They simply won't come back. Then they'll tell everyone else about it and give their business to your competitors.

Advanced Show and Tell

Do you remember "Show and Tell" day when you were in school? You were excited to bring in that great souvenir you got on vacation or the new toy you'd received for your birthday. Every child in your class was anxious for their turn to show-and-tell, but most kids didn't really pay attention to anything except for the items they considered were the "cool stuff." There was a lot of showing and telling, but not always a great deal of listening. Rarely did anyone ask questions.

Showing and telling is also about effective listening. Not only do you show customers your product and the value it will bring them, but you also go one step further by encouraging the customer to give you feedback. You may have a new idea for a product or service and spend a lot of time developing it—all in the interest of providing customers with what they want, but it may actually be something different. However, as part of your process of bringing new ideas to market, make a habit of getting input from your customers.

Arrange time to show your customers prototypes of new products or explain and demonstrate new services. They'll let you know if you're heading in the right direction or even tell you how you might improve your designs. Nothing is worse than spending a lot of time and money in product development, only to end up delivering something that doesn't meet the customers needs or, worse, something in which the customer has little interest.

Talk to Me!

When meeting with a group of customers to get their feedback, there are a few simple things you can do to make the most of the experience. Following are methods to help you in this process.

- ### Get ready to listen

   Before meeting with your customer, (or group of customers) determine what you want to accomplish. Are you looking for their reaction to a proposed idea? Are you interested in their perceptions of your current business? Are you trying to get to the heart of a difficult service issue? When you invite your customers to meet with you, let them know ahead of time what kind of information you're looking for. That way, they'll know ahead of time what they need to think about or research before your meeting. Perhaps they will need to review their maintenance logs, pull out records or talk to their employees before the meeting.

- ### Get the right people in the room

   Make sure you have included the right people in the discussion. If the customer's front line employees are the users of your products and services, ask to speak to them. Perhaps you want to speak to their sales people, engineers, account reps, etc. Each of them may bring a different perspective. Ideally, you'll want different people in your own organization to be involved with those discussions as well. Those who design, sell, deliver, and service what you provide may benefit from hearing directly from the customer.

- ### Set the tone

   Get your customer in a talkative mood by setting the proper tone for your meeting. They may be hesitant to provide you with honest feedback if they have any negative comments. After all, if you've invited them to provide feedback, served them a meal, and treated them as VIPs, they may not wish to come forth with any negative remarks.

   You can overcome any reluctance by sincerely stating that you're looking for their honest feedback. You can create a positive environment by saying something like: "I'd like you to tell us exactly how you feel about our new on-line ordering system. We want to make sure that it helps us service you better, but we don't really know if it works for you unless you give us your feedback. It's in both of our interests to make sure the ordering system meets your standards, so please, be straight with us and tell us about your experience using our system."

- **Ask open-ended questions**

  When you need feedback, ask open-ended questions: Who, what, why, when, and how. These generally elicit more than a yes or no response and can uncover a customer's preferences or needs, thereby helping you respond better.

- **Take notes**

  As you listen to what a customer says, ask questions and take orderly notes. Before leaving, review your notes and clarify any details. Keep in mind that as in your school days, you can walk out of a class with dozens of pages of notes and still have very little idea about what was said. If you were planning, or are planning to meet with a group of customers, it would be to your advantage to have someone other than yourself record the discussion on a laptop so that you can remain focused and facilitate the discussion. Remember that note-taking should be a supplement to good listening, not a replacement.

- **Listen objectively**

  As you listen to your customer, maintain an attitude of objectivity. This simply means you approach the situation with an open mind. In other words, wait and see what they have to say. If you're asking for difficult feedback, you may get an answer that's difficult to handle. Your first reaction may be to become defensive and try to explain your rationale. Remember: you're there to listen, not to defend.

  For instance, if a customer complains that it takes two weeks to receive a shipment from you instead of seven business days as promised, your reaction might be to say, "We don't have the room to keep excess inventory in our warehouse. Once we get an order, we manufacture the product, and that takes time." Your customer doesn't care about your capacity issue. All they care about is that they have to wait two weeks for their order rather than seven days.

- **Punch it out**

  When your customers finish talking, be sure to take the time to summarize what they have said, and while they're still there, create a "punch list" in as many categories as appropriate. This demonstrates that you understand what you have heard and are clear on what you have to do. It also gives you a list of ideas on which you can apply the creativity techniques we discussed earlier.

Involving customers in this manner will help obtain good feedback and demonstrate you have indeed listened and understood their concerns. Of course, it goes without saying that once you have obtained their input, then you need to act upon it. Nothing is more frustrating than to ask for your customers' suggestions but do nothing with the information. Your customer will give you great input about what you need to do, but fixing problems and figuring how to make their ideas a reality is up to you.

- **Turn to their turf**

Today, many savvy companies are inviting customers to their own headquarters in an attempt to "get close" to them, get their ideas and opinions on current and future products, and learn about their level of customer service satisfaction. This is an effective way to develop customer relationships, but I have found that if you want to hear the most powerful insights, meet on their turf. Meeting with your customers and potential customers on their own ground is a better environment for them to be more honest and spontaneous. It will also give you an opportunity to meet their people and see firsthand how your products and services are being used. Be sure to introduce yourself to as many people as you can while you're there to promote goodwill.

- **Make a "wish list"**

Excellent customer service is the key to building customer loyalty, but all the excellent service in the world won't mean a thing if you simply don't provide a product or service to the customer that he or she values. So, how do you know what customers want? Ask them. One simple process is to ask your customers to list the top five products and services that are most important to them. Next, record their most frequent answers. Then, take the top 20 percent of the suggestions given, and ask all your customers to prioritize them again. Then gear your products and services to what your customers value most. In this way, you can find out if what you think is in sync with what your customers think. You must offer products and services desired by customers so they perceive that you provide more value than the competition.

- **Take it seriously**

You'll realize the importance of listening to the customer if you think back on the times you encountered poor customer service and couldn't get anyone to listen to you, or when you purchased an expensive item and no one called to ask how you liked it. Those times demonstrated that you, the customer, don't matter. If you expect your business to thrive, you cannot afford to tune out the customer's voice. Don't take it for granted. Listening to your customer doesn't put you ahead of the game. It simply keeps you in the game.

Chapter 9

For Sales Professionals Only ... Sell Like There's No Tomorrow!

You've just spent all morning making cold calls and most often the result was an annoying voice-mail message. Those few live human beings who happened to pick up their phone responded indifferently with, "Well, send me some information." You recognize this as a blow-off and figure your expensive marketing materials will simply end up in a file somewhere or a secretary will throw it in the trash before anyone ever sees it. You ask yourself, "What does it take to get an appointment with a prospect? What good does it do to have excellent products and services if I can't even get in the door? What do I have to do to gain interest?"

Your spirits are down and your frustration level is high. You realize the result of the appointments you had earlier that week had also ended in rejection. You think about those sales goals you were hoping to exceed—especially after that rousing sales conference last month when management made an announcement to everyone that the company needs to sell at higher margins. You head out to lunch, hoping the afternoon will be more promising.

Here's a "wake up call" that an Achiever would not need: Having a state of mind such as the one I just described will not increase your sales ... but it will drain your energy! One of the many lessons you may need to remember from your Sales 101 training, besides "mirroring the customer," developing rapport, overcoming objections and having a smile on your face when speaking to prospects on the phone, etc. is this: If you aren't getting rejected two out of every three times, you're not trying hard enough. (And, as my colleague Jeffrey Gitomer, author of *The Sales Bible* says, "If you're getting rejected three out of three times, there's something seriously wrong!") This is a vital selling principle, for if you allow rejection to pull you down, you'll end up in a very poor frame of mind for any sales professional. Worse, you'll set yourself up to lose to some competitor who doesn't give up.

Achiever sales professionals would react by telling themselves, "Cold-calling is a numbers game. I usually average four for thirty-five. If I keep working hard, approach each call as if it will be the one that will get me in the door, then I'll get those new appointments. And, if I keep going back to those customers who rejected me and keep my foot in the door, and work to develop a good relationship with them, I'll eventually get them." (There's that positive attitude again.)

Most likely you've attended a Sales 101 course and learned many important selling skills, but you're in today's real world now. Increasing numbers of companies and individuals are making their purchases directly via the Internet, direct mail, telephone, and fax. These are some reasons why today's sales professionals are considered to be a whole new breed. And as I said earlier, they are required to do so much more than sell—they must bring *value* to the table. Today's companies and customers want Achievers who are more polished, have more expertise and are more effective in sales than ever before.

This chapter will identify how to handle rejection and address what I believe are the most important techniques—including some you'll remember from Sales 101 that, if practiced, will help you to meet and exceed your sales goals.

Know Your Odds in the Game

The first lesson you need to learn when facing frequent rejection is to know your batting average. Sales achievers know their odds. Just like a pitcher must know the batting average of the batter he faces before he throws the ball, you need to determine your batting average. Analyze your prospect-to-sale ratio. Let's say you average one sale for every eight prospects. If that seems typical, then you need to accept that you may have to hear an average of seven "No's" before you'll hear that "YES!" The old saying: "Sales is a numbers game" still holds true, even in today's real world. Always strive to improve your ratio, and keep in mind that, in many fields, generating one sale takes a large number of leads.

One of my clients is a provider of media content for web sites—news, business updates, stock-quotes, sports, photos, etc. When I asked their sales manager what she wanted me to reinforce in their sales training program, she replied, "I want them to realize that often they need to make fifty calls before they find someone who's interested in our services." How true.

If you find your average is suddenly much higher—for example, instead of eight contacts, it now takes you twenty to make a sale—then there may be a problem you need to address. Rejection is omnipresent in sales and should never be taken personally ... as long as you're certain you've done your very best.

Don't Give Up Too Easily

Many sales professionals face frequent rejection because they throw in the towel too soon. This is often due to impatience or a deflated ego. If a prospect doesn't buy after four or five calls, they take it personally and stop calling. Or, they may feel the prospect is loyal to the competitor and it's almost impossible to break through. Perhaps they think they can't beat low-price competition. None of these are good reasons to throw in the towel. A sharp sales professional needs to "reject rejection" and continue to pursue the customer.

Wake Up Again

Wake up and smell the competition! Rejecting rejection, playing the numbers game and good old persistence all count—but maybe it's time to try a *different approach*. If you're selling the same old way you have always sold and not getting the results you'd like, it's time to apply creativity to your approach. Just as companies need to differentiate themselves from their competitors, so must you. You must develop your own selling uniqueness and style and use it to your advantage.

Use Creativity and Be Tenacious

Think about it. Are you like every other salesperson who says, "May I send information for your review and follow up with a phone call?" Or worse, "Did you get our brochure?" Or, "I was wondering if you had a chance to look at my proposal." Or, if you work in retail, do you say the same thing every single retail salesperson in the world says: "May I help you?" Boring! If you find yourself saying these things or anything similar, it's time to use some creativity and improve your tenacity. If you say and do the same things as every other salesperson, how will you ever stand out in the customer's mind? By the way, if you hold a position in a retail store, why not say, "Hi. I'm Carol. I bet you're just looking. Be sure to check out the bargain table straight down the center aisle. Please ask for me if I can answer any questions for you."

Following are examples of how salespeople used creativity and tenacity to get new business. While some people used simple, fairly conservative approaches, others took a risk to be different. After all, no risk—no reward, right? Here's what they all share in common— each provided SALES RESULTS:

- **Coffee and donuts**

  A salesman for a printing company specializing in printing corporate annual reports had been trying for months to close a deal on a new account that would mean a large commission. He knew the decision-maker arrived at the office at 6:00 a.m. before everyone else and that he loved a particular brand of coffee and donuts. After an encouraging visit, he sent a messenger to the customer's office at 6:00 a.m. the next morning with a dozen fresh donuts and his favorite coffee served in a thermal jug which had the customer's name engraved on it. The attached card read: "If we can get you your coffee hot, and your doughnuts fresh, imagine what we can do for your printing needs." He got the deal!

- **Sell the pants off people**

  Creativity can also be used to get a sales position. Mark LeBlanc, a highly successful, small business marketing consultant, told me about how, as a young man he once took a chance to land a job. When he arrived in Saint Cloud, Minnesota to attend college in 1982, he had no money and no place to live. He went to a local church where the priest agreed to put him up for a couple nights. He knew he absolutely must find employment fast or he would become desperate. The next day, he went to a clothing store and applied for a sales position.

Since the store was short-handed on the day he applied, the manager had to constantly stop the interview in order to help customers. At one point, when the manager stepped outside his office to assist a customer, Mark looked out into the store and noticed a gentlemen in the deserted Men's Department. Without hesitating, he went over to the man and said, "Those pants are terrific and if you want to try them on, you can use the dressing room over there."

The man thanked Mark and went to try on the pants. Then Mark quickly found the manager, who by this time had already noticed what was going on. He asked the manager what the store's alteration policies were and went back to help the customer. The customer bought two pairs of pants. The owner hired Mark on the spot.

Mark's case, while not exactly an example of how to sell a particular product or service, does show how to sell perhaps the most important commodity of all: yourself, for if you can't sell yourself, how can you sell anything else?"

- **Trade show success: ya gotta have a gimmick**

A colleague of mine, Doug Dvorak, was Regional Sales Director for Boca Research, a data communications hardware manufacturer. His company attended the world's largest computer show, COMDEX. This international trade show is held in Las Vegas every fall and easily attracts over 3 million people in a one-week period. This particular year, Doug was charged with running the Boca booth. In addition to all the other duties associated with show set-up and booth management, he was also assigned to provide an interesting giveaway item to attract people to their booth.

Doug put on his creative sales hat and thought long and hard about what would be an innovative, creative, and cost-effective way to get client and media attention. He had been racking his brain one evening and came up with only a few lackluster concepts, so he took a break and went out to dinner and a movie with his wife and some close friends. After dinner, they had some time to kill before the movie started so they went for a walk. They happened across a novelty store, wandered in and took a look around. One particular item caught Doug's eye—a propeller beanie sitting on a shelf between a pair of Groucho Marx glasses and a bucket full of unidentifiable gadgets. This was an absurd little hat—too small to fit a typical human head—with a propeller boldly affixed to the top. Doug's creative intuition told him he must wear this cap. To the chagrin of his wife, he wandered around the store looking like a complete fool, but was struck by a thought: "Technical people are commonly referred to as 'Propeller Heads.' Maybe there's a tie-in!"

To Doug, this wouldn't be just a new way to amuse himself and embarrass his wife, this would be an excellent industry-relevant gimmick! After checking into the price, he realized this was too good to pass up. He decided to order a gross and emboss the phrase "The Boca Beanie" across the front and give them to current and potential clients.

Doug was amazed by the overwhelmingly positive response. Clients were falling all over themselves spinning the little propellers absurdly standing atop their heads. He relayed this information to his company's marketing department and after some further consideration, they chose to follow his idea and purchased 25,000 propeller beanies. (I can imagine how hard it must have been for Doug to urge a dignified company to purchase 25,000 beanies with a straight face!) He said that when he and his sales team started giving them away at the show, the response was overwhelming. Boca had the hottest giveaway and the most booth traffic at the show. Lines of people sneaked through the floor of the presentation hall, blocking other booths, waiting to get to the Boca display to get their hands on the Boca Beanie. As Doug frantically tried to demonstrate his products to the overwhelming number of people crowded around him and give away the Boca Beanies, he yelled, "Don't look like a moron, get your free Boca Beanie today!" (Now THAT took guts!) It wasn't long before the media got wind of the Beanie. Before Doug was done spinning his propeller, he was interviewed on the *CBS Evening News* with Dan Rather, featured in *USA Today* and highlighted in all the industry trade publications.

Doug told me it was doubtlessly the most effective sales gimmick he had ever employed—simple, fun and a little wacky. Most important, the inquiries and sales orders that followed were highly impressive!

Inspiration strikes at the oddest times—you can't force a great idea, it's born from your creativity and attention to the world around you.

- **Don't let customers fly the coop**

A colleague told me about a friend's father who was a sales-man in the New York garment industry. He had failed at every attempt to get an appointment with the owner of a big retail store. Not wanting to give up, he sent a messenger to promptly and care-fully bring the owner a very special gift in a box. The messenger was told to deliver it *only* to the owner and be very careful with the package. Having no way to get around receiving the gift in person, the owner came out, picked up the box, and signed for it.

He was surprised to notice that the box had several small holes and something was moving inside. When he opened it, he found a docile messenger pigeon inside with a capsule tied to its leg. The message in the capsule said, "If you don't want to give me an ap-pointment, don't let this pigeon return home."

The salesman was delighted to see the pigeon return to its roost barely an hour after the messenger left. He realized how quickly the owner must have opened his office window to send the pigeon home. He picked up his samples with a grin on his face, and left for his appointment.

Granted, these examples are rather unusual, but I wanted to dem-onstrate that with a little creativity it's possible to get a potential customer's attention. Of course, you must use an approach that's comfortable and fits with your personality and your customer's per-sonality. For example, if you have a no-nonsense, no sense of humor customer, or if you're in an industry where the nature of the business is more serious, you need to be conservative with your approach. But remember—even though you may need to be conservative, strive to be different and memorable in a positive way.

Go for the Gold When Prospecting

Prospects—where to find them! If you're a small business owner or have a sales position in a small company, prospects can come from numerous and varied sources. If you consistently keep your antennae out, you'll find them everywhere. You simply need to have a mindset that *everyone* is a prospect until you find out otherwise. For example, one of the most successful real estate agents I've ever met acquired a good deal of business from his health club. Right after he joined, he quickly made friends with the receptionist, gave her a few business cards, and told her that if she knew of anyone who wanted to buy or sell a home, he'd be grateful if she'd give them his card. Each day when he worked out on the exercise machines or jogged around the track, he small-talked with everyone he could and made sure he would tactfully shift the conversation to "Are you interested in selling your house somewhere down the road?" And, "Have you seen the property for sale over on Lincoln Avenue? It's a real bargain and the house is immaculate. Why don't you take a look?" He acquired many contacts and made many sales this way.

He's not the only one I know who has found their health club to be a source of leads. A landscaping contractor told me that during the winter months, (I live in Chicago, remember) he spends a good deal of time at his health club to "schmooze" with prospective clients. He claims he has gotten many new accounts using this method. A construction contractor met my friend Barbara at their health club and ended up building a large addition to her home. My friend Charlene, the owner of a successful staffing firm, makes it a point to work out at her health club during the busiest times for the obvious reason.

Health clubs are only one non-traditional source to acquire leads for small businesses, but there are many others: golf courses, the hair salon, Starbucks, airports, and any functions where you can network. If you really want to sell, you can find potential leads in many places. Just as long as you aren't pushy in your approach, it's legal! Didn't Sales 101 teach you that you must be 100 percent sales-minded everywhere you go? Get on the phone. Get in your car and go to the places where people need your product or service. And remember: EXTROVERTS RULE!

If you represent a mid-size or large organization, the best sources for prospecting are the Internet, your customers and your suppliers. Master the Internet and use it to arm yourself with industry knowledge and seek new business. It's the best way to stay ahead in the game. You can find leads on the Internet by applying the same techniques we discussed in the "Know Your Competition" chapter.

How's your ability to get referral leads? Every customer knows a customer you need to know. Getting referral business is the least expensive way to get new customers, and has the highest leverage and potential payoff. And, a customer who buys because you came to them through a referral is less likely to price-shop.

Challenge yourself to ask for as many referrals as you can. However, if you're already skilled at it, you know that getting one good one is always better than having hundreds of names in your database. The way to get that cherished golden lead is this: the better your sales technique, the harder you work, and the more likable you are, the more referral leads you'll acquire. If you've been serving and helping your customers and are well liked, it will eventually come to the attention of many people. Don't forget to send a handwritten note and a small token of appreciation to the person who gave you the referral if it results in business.

Rely on the wonderful software that's available today to track and control your leads. There simply is no better way to manage them. Categorize prospects whichever way works best for you. Depending on your product/service, one method you might want to consider is to use three categories:

- Hot, meaning ready to buy.
- Strong, meaning there's a strong chance you'll get a sale.
- Cool, meaning your chances of making a sale don't appear to be strong due to the fact that they either have expressed little interest or have not been receptive to numerous calls.

Don't be too quick to delete Cools from your database. If there's even a remote chance you may eventually get their business, don't give up. The serendipity of the universe has blessed many a salesperson with orders from customers that they never expected. So continue to call them from time to time. You just never know when they will be receptive, when a different approach may work or when they may have left the company and you can start fresh with a new buyer.

Qualify

You need to be proficient at qualifying a buyer and have a polished approach. Make sure you have it down and that you sound professional, confident, conversational and natural—as if it's second nature to you. It's also critical to know as much as you can about their business before you call.

But is your sales success based solely on your prospecting numbers? If you care only about the quantity of sales calls you make, and not the quality of the calls, you'll jeopardize your ability to make quota. Your goal is to get to the decision-maker and find out if he or she has the need and the dollars to buy your product. Finding the *right* person to talk to will save you from wasting valuable time. If you can't get to the decision-maker after a few attempts, befriend the Gatekeeper. Call them by their first name, and use phrases such as, "Would you be so kind to help me out a little ...." (The next section offers more effective words and phrases.) Probe deeply when you speak to the decision-maker, and strive to make an appointment where you can put on a presentation under ideal conditions.

Prospecting and qualifying are of primary importance, but remember, don't let the number of prospects in your database impress you. The only numbers that count are your sales revenues.

Clearly Define your Product, Its Benefits, and Why a Customer Should Give You and your Company their Business.

WHY should a customer do business with your company? Sales success requires that you can communicate to the customer that what you offer provides *value* to them. Hopefully, the company you represent has a reputation for product and service quality and are able to boast a proven track record of on-time delivery (that's a given). They should have an impressive number of loyal customers and stand behind their products. They should conduct market research and stay on top of trends while constantly improving the features of their product or service.

You need to make sure you know your company's distinctive competence. For example, you may be considered a leader in your industry, be capable of handling complex projects and have the capacity to meet an increased demand. You may provide expertise in designing or manufacturing complicated parts or products. You may offer both after-the-sale and technical support that exceeds the expectations of your existing customers. Perhaps you can handle large accounts promptly but devote equal attention to smaller accounts. If your company is smaller than your competitor's, you can emphasize that you can provide more personalized service.

Maybe your company is considered by others in your industry to be a "world class" manufacturer. Possibly, you offer a written money-back guarantee. Perhaps you're a sole-distributor or small business that can offer something your competitors cannot. All of these are reasons why a customer should do business with your company. Remember: customers buy success. Your company's success can lead to their success ... and that can lead to their loyalty to you. They also buy your reputation and other people's opinions of it. That's why testimonials are great sales ammunition.

Next, WHY will a customer benefit from your product or service? It's not enough to have product knowledge, but you need to clearly articulate the benefits your product or service can provide. So ask yourself, what are the real benefits—not features now—but *benefits*) Then, determine how those benefits translate into *value* to the customer—improved productivity, increased profitability, greater efficiency, or solve a problem? Will it reduce procurement expenses? Can it provide peace of mind? Can it reduce floor space, cut the number of suppliers, or reduce parts numbers or labor costs? Does it provide reduction in inventory or cut setup and changeover times? Do you customize and offer options? Do you offer personalized shopping? Do you offer a customer-loyalty program that can save them money? All of these and more are reasons why a customer will benefit from buying what you offer.

Last, WHY should a customer do business with you? An ideal model of a sales professional is one who is knowledgeable, (I mean one who really *knows* their product and industry) is honest, has integrity, follows through on commitments, is personable, and has a sense of humor. The customer must have confidence in them, be able to trust them and know they can solve problems for them. They must feel valued and that the salesperson is not in business for his or herself—but is in business to help the customer. They must be made to feel like a VIP from the get-go. If these things can be said about you and your customer feels this way, you're in good shape.

Hopefully, you were able to affirm all of the above. Now here are the critical questions you must ask yourself if you want to win the order: Are you conveying this information to customers and making it sound real? Do you believe your product or service is the best in the business and extremely valuable to the customer? Do you guide your prospect to an understanding about your products and services? Do you believe your whole purpose is to serve customers effectively? If you do, it will come through loud and clear.

Communication is key. You must be able to communicate with confidence WHY customers should do business with YOU, WHY your product and service is superior and WHY customers can depend on your company. You must be able to convey it to them and make it real. Combine your understanding of this process with what customers want and they will buy from you. As you communicate your value, strive to be conversational in your approach, and above all make it clear that you want to help the customer. Be clear, concise, and brief. Do not oversell and shut up when you get the order. Remember to be sincere, and if you're speaking the truth, it will bring results.

Ask Questions and LISTEN

I often wonder why more companies don't train their people in listening skills, for it's the only means by which you can learn what a customer's needs really are. Many salespeople think it's important for them to talk, talk, talk. However, they're losing sales because they're talking when they should be listening. They just don't get it! They need to learn that they can impress the customer by using their EARS not their mouth. They think, "How can I sell myself, my product, and my customer if I'm not talking." Of course, it's important to explain these things to the customer, but customers need you to listen to *their* concerns. They want to make sure that you understand *their* needs, priorities and expectations. If you don't listen, they'll find someone else who does.

Listening is a function of asking. In your initial meeting, ask good solid questions such as, "How's your business?" "What's important to you about …?" "What do you want to accomplish?" "What's your application?" "Why are you considering this project?" Ask those open-end type questions and take careful notes as we talked about in the "Listen to Your Customer" chapter. And remember: Rarely will you ever listen yourself out of a customer. Ask questions to learn about your prospect's desires, needs, and fears, and you'll know how to position your product or service where it will be perceived as being critical to your customer's success.

Memorize Responses to Objections

You've given an excellent sales presentation, and the customer jumps up and shouts, "Where do I sign?" Of course, it never works that way. Customers will have questions, objections and concerns about your product or service. They're making a major decision and want to be sure it's the best one. When a customer objects, make sure you uncover the real objection. Is it about price, quality, service, capacity, etc.?

Before you meet with a customer, think about the company's situation, its needs and its issues in relationship to what you provide. Where might any objections arise? Prepare for every possible objection they may make and *memorize* responses to them. Better yet, don't wait for them to be raised. Incorporate answers to common objections into your sales presentation. This will demonstrate you're in touch with the customer's situation.

"Your price is too high!" is an objection you may hear often. Don't jump in and defend your price. You can't win when you're on the defensive and your prospect may interpret your quick response to be that your price *is* too high. You need to emphasize the value your product will bring to the customer and ask more questions. Give them facts related to buyer benefits and supportive evidence to convince them they're justified in buying. Speak in terms of positive outcomes for your customer. If done correctly, you can turn the objection around.

Respond to objections with assertiveness. I want to stress that assertiveness does not mean aggressiveness. People tend to equate the two. You'd be amazed at how effective you can be with a soft-spoken approach with a confident manner. Sounding confident about what you're selling can make the difference between success and failure.

Use the verbal cushions you'll learn in the next section and practice your responses to objections until they're burned into your brain. Your motivation to practice them is not only your commission-check, but by recognizing that your sale helps provide a paycheck for everyone in your company. And, *that* is why all who are employed by your organization should do everything to support your sales efforts.

Ask Already! Then Seal the Deal.

Here's another Sales 101 principle: The "ABC" acronym for "Always Be Closing." All too often, sales representatives, retail salespeople and small business owners present their ideas and information flawlessly, and then hesitate, or worse, neglect to ask for the sale. They give the presentation and then wait for the customer to say, "Okay, we'll get back to you." Ask for the business and close! When you're uncomfortable with asking for the deal and hesitate, you have just made it easy for them to say "no thank you." If your product or service truly meets the customer's needs and you've presented it well, they'll be inclined to buy but you still need to hook them.

Watch their body language. Ask for the order as soon as you notice positive buying signals such as head nodding, or if they're rubbing their chin because they're probably contemplating the order. Ask! If they listen to everything you have to say and ask, "What's the price?" or "How long for delivery?" those questions are also buying signals. Being sensitive to these signals and jumping in at this point to ask for the sale will increase your sales and commission income.

Ask your customer a closing question such as, "Do you feel we're in line with your needs and this will meet your objectives?" If they say yes, ask for the order! Then simply say, "Are you ready to move on this?" or, "Shall we place the order?" or, "Seems we're on target with your needs. Would you like me write it up?" (Be sure to say it in one breath.)

If they're not in a position to make a decision while sitting with you, that's okay. Bigger decisions do require more thought. Get a commitment for action. Politely ask permission to call in a couple of days or ask when they'll make a decision and point out that you're available if they have any questions later.

Follow Up

Now you've left the customer's office, pleased that you've given a great presentation. They seemed impressed and said they'll be making a decision by the end of the week. You've done your best, so sit back and wait for the call, right? Wrong! You need to follow up with the customer within the next day or two. You aren't calling to push for a decision; that only makes people uncomfortable. Rather, you want to say, "I enjoyed meeting with you, and just wanted to give you a quick call to see if you had any questions or concerns at this time."

This will show the customer that you're polite, conscientious and most of all, that you're indeed working to establish a relationship.

What do most sales professionals do after a presentation? They call in a couple of days and say, "I was wondering if you thought about ..." How common! Do you want to be *different*? Send an attention getting fax (E-mail will get read and disappear into Cyberspace) use phrases that describe the "WHY'S" we discussed earlier. Following are good examples"

"I've given further thought to your needs. You need to ..."

"XYZ is one of the most respected ..."

"We're a top rated ..."

"We're considered a leader in ..."

"We have won the business and respect of ..."

"We're considered the preferred supplier of . . ."

"We offer the added advantage of ..."

"We're dedicated to ..."

"We recognize the realities/importance of ..."

"We have a proven track record of on-time delivery and we stand behind our work."

Next, make a few statements about their needs and how your product or service will benefit them:

"Our product is designed for today's ..."

"You'll be able to ..."

"Our clients tell us they have increased ..."

Conclude with why they should give you the order: "I'm confident you'll be more than pleased with the level of service you'll receive in working with myself and everyone at XYZ. I would welcome the opportunity to be your supplier. Please contact me if you have any further questions or if I can be of service in any way. I assure you of my attention at all times."

Now that's class! Just be sure you compose your communication in a style that fits your customer.

The "Like" Factor

Remember, success in sales is not only due to the quality of your products and services, the brilliance of your sales presentation, or even luck. More often it's the "like factor." Great sales trainers will tell you that customers are not always buying your product or service; more often, they're buying YOU. It's your personality and how you conduct yourself that become major factors in the decision. Keep in mind that people want to enjoy the buying experience. You must come across as likable, genuine, sincere, helpful, trustworthy and amiable. Each encounter with a customer, whether in person, on the phone, or electronic, must have interaction that is pleasing.

Earlier, I emphasized the importance of trusting your intuition. I recommend that you keep this in mind: People get a "gut-feeling" about you when they meet you in person for the first time. Make sure it's a positive first impression. Project an air of confidence without arrogance. Refrain from badmouthing the competition or it will show you lack class. If you turn customers off, they'll look elsewhere. You don't make the sale by attacking the competition; you make the sale by working hard for it, proving yourself and by portraying a higher class of service in every aspect of the selling cycle.

Here's another tip you need to remember: If you can make your customer *laugh*, you'll have a better chance of making a sale.

Develop Strong Customer Relationships

If you're in a business where a customer will not likely purchase often, such as a car dealership, a mortgage lender, or real estate broker, be sure to build relationships and create goodwill by communicating often with them after a purchase. Whether it's a simple written note, a phone call, or e-mail, those extra touches make them feel special. Your effort will pay off with greater loyalty.

Selling is all about developing relationships. Inga, a real estate broker, has achieved success in selling homes because she works hard to develop relationships. She told me about how she had sold a house belonging to an older couple that moved from Chicago to Florida to enjoy their retirement in the warm weather. She called them at least twice a year to say hello and ask how they were doing. Three years later, she received a call from them asking her to contact their daughter and her husband. They were living in Chicago and wanted to sell their existing home and purchase a larger one. Inga listed their daughter's house, sold it, and then helped them buy a larger home in an exclusive area. A great Return on Investment for the time it took Inga to make those two phone-calls per year.

You need to establish long-term relationships with customers and potential customers. This is important if you want to make more than just the initial sale. For many sales professionals, there is a need to establish a solid relationship with them long before they can make the first sale. Position yourself as an ongoing, valuable resource to customers by providing them with ideas and information you think they can use. Get to know their business and what's important to them.

I'm reminded of a particular consulting arm of one of the big eight accounting firms. When their people work with a client, they make it a priority to learn as much about the client's business as possible. While working with a major corporation on a large project, their consulting team became such a valuable resource that some of the corporation's internal departments who could provide the same service found themselves left out of the loop. Their own corporate team didn't know their own company's business as well as the accounting firm's team. No wonder it was easy for the consulting firm to sell their services on this project.

You need to be actively engaged in your customers' business and they must be made to feel you're "partnering" with them to help them achieve their goals. This holds true even when you're unable to help them. In my sales seminars, I remind people to help the customer in every way possible. That may mean referring them to another company that *can* meet their needs when you are unable. This clearly demonstrates you have the customer's best interest in mind and helps develop the relationship. When was the last time you helped a customer when there was nothing in it for you?

Part of establishing and building strong relationships is developing these effective partnerships. *They exist when you want the same things for your customers that they want for themselves.* You must internalize the customer's goals and make them your own. When customers know you have their interests at heart and they see that you've tied your success to their own, they'll know that you're serious about partnering with them. Effective partnerships help maintain the loyalty of your customers—a topic we'll address in our next chapter.

Be Boldly Honest

The most important ingredient of any relationship—whether business or personal—is a shared sense of trust. You cannot be successful in any relationship without it because trust is the foundation for reliability, dependability, honesty and good faith. That's why it's critical to be up front and honest from Day One. When something goes wrong, honesty is always the best policy.

A former headhunter told me that during the 1980s, he'd accepted a consulting role with a sporting goods equipment manufacturer and received a retainer to find a technology director for their equipment division in western Michigan. This was at a time when the frontiers of local computing and use of personal computers were just coming into their own. The company realized the potential value that could be realized if bowling enthusiasts were able to have their scoring electronically processed. There were also electronic gains to be made, perhaps through the use of robotics for mechanical operations and through use of computers to automate many of the management tasks that were currently being done manually. He told me how he'd searched high and low for the right person to head up the task of introducing electronics and computing into bowling for his client. He said he kept running into the same problem again and again and it seemed no one wanted to move their family into the technology backwaters of western Michigan for fear that they would quickly become too specialized and their knowledge would become obsolete.

After several months of work where one promising candidate after another considered the job and then backed out, he was asked by senior management at corporate headquarters to come in to report on his work. He said that his gut instinct at that morning meeting—which would be attended by the division general manager and the corporation's vice president of human resources—was to give a glowing report of undefined progress and to waffle, but he decided otherwise.

At the meeting he would have liked to be able to report substantial progress, and being close to completion of a task he had by then already been fully paid to do. Instead, he confessed that he'd run into one dead end after another, and had no good prospects to report to date. He was honest, transparent and revealing. He expected to encounter dismay and dissatisfaction, and that could end this valued client relationship.

Instead, the vice president of human resources laughed aloud and said, "Thank God someone else has the same problems that we've had." He went on to recount several similar disappointments in his own experience in trying to fill jobs at that particular location.

Instead of losing a major client, my friend left with two new assignments and a much closer business relationship. Despite all the pessimism many of us have encountered before and since about the need for sales people to control the information given to customers, this is a clear example of why I always have believed that bold honesty pays.

Promise only what you can deliver and deliver what you promise. It's that simple. If you're only thinking about bottom lines, profit margins and increased sales as you interact with customers, then you'll never be truly successful.

Conquer Selling Slumps

I work with many sales groups who want to know what to do when they're experiencing a "selling slump." A decline in sales makes both the salesperson and their company *vulnerable* to the competition.

Let's first define what I mean by a selling slump. I'm not referring to frequent rejection, but to what happens when your sales have been down for weeks at a time. What should you do when this happens? Say, "To hell with it" and go play golf? Jump ship? Eat chocolate? Slit your wrist?

If you're an Achiever (Yes, even Achievers can run into a slump), you instinctively know you must press on and continue "dialing for dollars" to existing and potential customers to get yourself out of a negative sales period. You may also need to consider using a new approach and look carefully at your sales strategies, strengths, and weaknesses.

Following are areas you may need to think about which may have contributed to your current situation and help you to prevent selling slumps in the future. (Even if you're meeting or exceeding your sales goals you can benefit by reviewing this.)

- **Shield yourself from negative emotions**

First, avoid giving in to negative emotions if sales have been down for a period of time. If you begin thinking that you won't make a sale, then you probably won't. If customers sense your apprehension or pessimism, then they'll look toward another company who is more confident. Sound optimistic and convincing. You need to act like a winner, even if you haven't won the race for a while. Just like a thoroughbred who wears blinders to keep his eyes on the finish line without getting distracted, you must forge ahead on "blind-faith" that business will turn around ... and it will.

- **Enthusiasm**

What's your level of enthusiasm these days? Do you still have that same enthusiasm you once had when you got your first job? You remember that, don't you? You were ready to conquer the world! Remember: There's no mystical, magical secret to sales success. It comes from the enthusiasm you display when you believe in yourself, your company, its products and its people. Enthusiasm is contagious and, when you're enthusiastic, your customers will feel that same way and give you their business.

- **Spend your time effectively**

Are you spending too much time going after small accounts, without consistently striving to get business from larger accounts? Remember the 80/20 rule: "20 percent of your customers will generate 80 percent of your business." Are you going after the right 20 percent every day? Have you thrown in the towel too easily with this valuable potential business? Would just a few more chances at bat give you the home run?

Your phone's not ringing? How many calls are you making? If there aren't enough incoming calls, there must not be enough going out! Muster up the discipline to spend several hours on the phone each day to help generate business and get you out of the quicksand and onto solid selling ground. I learned this from Ken Keller whom I consider to be one of the best salesmen I've ever known. He owns a training and development company where I had a part-time position in sales before my speaking career. He always told us that if the phones were quiet, it was because the sales team was not making enough calls. I still remember that no matter whether business was slightly down or whether they had more than they could handle, he always had the discipline to get on the phones and hustle business each day as if there was no tomorrow!

- **Positive energy**

  I learned long ago that if you want to be successful at anything, you not only need a positive attitude but you also need a great deal of physical energy to go with it. There's just no way you can accomplish anything—let alone beat the competition in today's world—without it. Be sure to get enough sleep and watch your alcohol intake so that you'll be in top condition to sell—especially before a big trade show, convention, annual meeting, crucial customer meeting or any function that requires you to "gear up." I also encourage you to incorporate the self-management practices in Section 4. If you do, your level of energy will soar.

- **Invest in yourself**

  There's one more thing you MUST do to get yourself out of a selling slump and prevent them from recurring: Spend increasing amounts time and energy on self-improvement. Study and apply the skills in this book. Take a refresher course on sales training, or enroll in an advanced sales training program.

  Ask yourself how much time you're spending in this critical area. If you're not spending enough, make it a priority in your life to be dedicated to continuous self-improvement and focused learning. You'll soon discover that it's worth the time and money you've invested and will pay off more than you may ever dream possible.

Born to Be in Sales?

Those who have acquired a high degree of proficiency in selling are often referred to as "born salespeople." They may be described as extroverted, persuasive, likable, and even charismatic. The truth is, these characteristics can only take you so far. Selling is an acquired skill. An Achiever salesperson has learned and *practiced* the fine art of selling so that it appears to others as if they have a natural talent for it.

Great salespeople were not born at the top. They clawed their way up like everyone else. Their proficiency came from constant trial and error, continuous practice and by being highly demanding of themselves. Funny thing about the top, though. It's not as small a space as you might think. Apply what you've learned, then get out there and sell like there's no tomorrow. I'll be there to meet you at the summit.

Chapter 10

Ditch Customer Satisfaction ...
Go for CUSTOMER LOYALTY

You shouted a huge "YES!" from your desk as you hung up the phone and heard the good news. You landed that new customer! You thought about all those sales calls, meetings, tough price negotiations and endless hours you had to endure to get that account. Your sales team gave you a "thumbs up" and joined you after work to celebrate your big victory. A great time was had by all.

While driving to the office the next morning, reality set in when you realized the real work has just begun. You successfully swayed the customer over to your company from your competitor even though like you, they also offer fair pricing, excellent service, and convenience. In fact, you recall reading a recent survey in a trade journal that touted your competitor's extremely high level of customer satisfaction. Yes, your company also has a great reputation and a high level of customer satisfaction, but now that you reeled in the new account you know your company must do everything possible to *keep* that customer.

There's no lock and key on them, as other competitors will attempt to do everything in their power to take this new account away from you, just like you took it away from one of them. In addition, your customer will be reviewing your pricing carefully and seeking bids from other competitors while they're doing business with you. You start to feel overwhelmed with all that it's going to take just to keep that customer. Besides, you know that, as a salesman, you're judged not only by how many sales you close, but also by how many sales lead to repeat business.

In the past, simply satisfying that customer may have been sufficient enough to keep them coming back for more business. More recently, taking actions to delight that customer was considered commendable. But which would you and your company rather have—one hundred satisfied customers or one hundred loyal customers? In today's real world, establishing customer loyalty must be your ultimate goal. You not only want the customer to continue to use your product or service without being tempted to sway over to a competitor, but you want them to spread the word to their associates about you.

It's well-known that it's cheaper to retain an existing customer than to acquire a new one. Loyal customers create a positive feedback loop, for the more revenue you can generate from a customer, the more funds your company can invest toward their marketing, advertising, new product development, etc. to help you in your sales efforts.

How do you establish customer loyalty when the whole world is circling in like a pack of wolves to get them too? You, and everyone in your company have to *earn* it.

Exceed Expectations

We've all heard a great deal about how we must take the "Extra Step" to exceed customer expectations. Even though we've all heard this, it warrants reinforcement. Exceeding customer expectations is more than just providing quality service. It's simply what we must do if we want customers to be loyal. Think for a moment about your auto mechanic, your tailor, or your favorite restaurant. Why are you a loyal customer? Is it because they provide fair pricing? Possibly. Is it because of their location? Maybe. Is it the quality of their product? Probably. Is it because their service exceeds your expectations? Most definitely. Chances are you genuinely like them as people, trust their expertise, and know you can rely on them to respond to your individual needs.

Recently, I purchased a spiffy new sports car from a dealership I located through the Internet. John, my salesman, had a laid-back selling style (rare for a car salesperson!) and spoke with sincerity. He took his time (or more importantly, let me take my time) and answered all my questions patiently. He treated me with the utmost professionalism. Because I trusted him, I gave him the sale. When I picked up the car the next day, he helped me remove my belongings from the glove compartment and the trunk of my old vehicle, (there sure was a lot of junk, I confess) and neatly transferred them into my new car. I most certainly did not expect that and he didn't have to do it. There were potential buyers in the showroom looking at the new cars. He could have been in a hurry to get me out of there but instead, he impressed me with his graciousness and made me feel important—a critical skill when dealing with any customer in any situation. A customer should always be treated as a VIP. I was extremely pleased that had given him the sale.

After driving the new car only two weeks, I managed to put a nasty scratch on the rear fender while lifting a heavy suitcase with metal wheels from the trunk. I was distraught that this had happened to my new car, but decided to hold off doing the body repair until my 3000-mile check up. When I arrived at the dealership for my first routine servicing, I said to the service manager and the body shop manager, "Can you believe I put this nasty scratch on this beautiful new car so soon after buying it? I can't drive a brand new sports car with a big scratch on it. What's it going to cost me to have it refinished?" They looked at each other and the body shop manager said, "Ms. Corelli, it's a shame this happened to you. Tell you what. This is your first service visit with us so this one's on the house."

Not only was I delighted, but I was thoroughly impressed once again! I certainly didn't expect them to do the bodywork for free. That's almost unheard of these days! But that wasn't all. Both the service manager and the bodyshop manager were genuine, gracious, and asked me several questions about how the car had been performing. When I told them that I was getting ready for a long road trip the service manager said, "Don't worry. We'll be sure your car is in top-notch condition before you hit the road." I felt really confident that they would, too.

I asked them how long it would take for the servicing and body repair, explaining that I had to get back to my office in a reasonable amount of time. They offered me a loaner car, but I told them I preferred to wait because it was a bit of a drive. They brought me over to the general manager and arranged for me to use the dealership's conference room so I could work on my laptop and make business calls from their phone. Before I knew it, there was a knock on the door and someone brought me a pot of coffee! Soon my car was brought up to the front of the dealership—clean, shiny and looking brand-new. The service manager opened the door for me and asked if I needed anything more. I was delighted. This certainly wasn't like the dealership where I bought my old car. There, the staff hurried me through and hustled me for unnecessary service add-ons.

Since my experience with this dealership, I've told many people about how I not only got the best deal from them, but how well they treat their customers. It was obviously a service excellent organization. I not only received superior service from John, the salesman, but everyone who worked there made me feel as if they cared about my satisfaction and went out of their way to please me. I'll be back there for my next car and will continue to tell anyone I know who's thinking about buying a new car about them. I am a loyal customer.

Larry Salani is a talented graphic artist who has designed my promotional materials for many years. There are many creative graphic artists out there, but more important to me, Larry is a hardworking, warm and genuine person who consistently demonstrates that he really cares about creating marketing materials that will help my business to grow. He not only understands how vital my promotional materials are to my business, but he recognizes that my personality is such that I need to be involved in the creative process. Whenever I have a new project, he allows me to sit next to him at his computer while he creates the artwork and design. I honestly don't know any other graphic artist who would do this. When his work is completed he helps me find the best printing deal and oversees the project himself. He calls me frequently to let me know the status of the job so I don't become anxious. He sends someone to deliver the printing that carries the heavy boxes to my second floor office and even places them on the proper shelf. After I work with the new materials a while, he phones me several times to see how my current and potential clients are reacting to them.

Larry calls me regularly to ask how my business is going and to offer assistance wherever he can. Over the years I've known him, his business has grown tremendously, and he now creates package designs for major retail organizations. As busy and successful as has he has become, he still continues to provide me with excellent service and exceeds my expectations. I have referred numerous clients to him. I am a loyal customer.

One of my clients is a manufacturer of air-conditioning equipment for specialized applications. Although their products are usually more costly to their customers (heavy-duty equipment manufacturers) than their competitors' they have a reputation for producing some of the highest quality air-conditioning equipment in the world. They invited me to a customer appreciation function where one of their clients from Milwaukee told me, "I love these guys. They do a good job for us and are always reliable. I may have to pay more for each unit, but our dealers tell us their customers rave about the efficiency of the equipment. In the long run, it's worth it to work with them. I wouldn't do business with any other firm unless I absolutely had to. They are definitely the best." He is a loyal customer.

So what do the car dealership, the graphic artist, and the manufacturer have in common? They all know what it takes to build customer loyalty. They know that getting business is one thing, keeping it is another. Your sales force needs to depend on everyone to provide quality service as a team and do everything possible to please the customer. This chapter will provide information to help you keep customers and make them loyal to you and your organization.

Establish a Quality Service Culture

As I said earlier, today's customers, whether they are direct consumer or business-to-business customers, first and foremost want to deal with organizations that have a good reputation. Thanks to the Internet, they talk to each other about whether they enjoyed their stay at your hotel in Boston, or whether your product does all your ad claims it will do. They want to be treated well and serviced by people who listen to them and care about them.

Every person who works for your company is a salesperson, even if they aren't responsible for selling the initial product or service to the customer. Customers are constantly evaluating your company and whether or not they will continue to do business with you. Anytime they have contact with anyone in your company for any reason, it's imperative that every person demonstrates care and concern. What kind of answers does the customer get when they contact your billing department? What does the shipping department do when the customer has a special request? How do your service technicians treat people when they go to the customer's office? How's their tone of voice? Do they sound like they're HAPPY to be servicing customers?

Everything your people say and do has an effect on customer loyalty. If they don't say and do the right things, they can destroy the reputation of your company as well as the relationship you have begun to build. As my colleague Sam Geist says, "Your people can be your ambassadors or your assassins." Everyone must understand the importance of customer service and consistently act as ambassadors who promote goodwill. They must realize that the customer is the person who creates and sustains their job. Every current and potential customer, whether they give you a great deal of business, or are a small account, should be treated as if they were Stradivarius violins—valuable, priceless, to be cherished and handled with delicacy. A Quality Service Culture must exist throughout your entire organization so that your employees seek out every opportunity where they can exceed customer expectations and provide total value before, during and after the sale.

Every person in your organization must commit to this if you want to establish customer loyalty. This holds true whether you have one person working for you or one thousand and more. The company's sales force needs to be able to depend on everyone to do everything possible to please the customer. As I said earlier, getting their business is one thing, keeping it is another. Below are some methods to help you to build a quality customer service culture in your company:

- *Create guiding principles for your company that require people to uphold core values of honesty, professionalism, ethics, integrity and caring.* Employees must be informed of this culture before they're hired and current employees need to be reminded of these guiding principles. Then you need to make sure your people continually exhibit these values.

- *Create a written service policy and reproduce it so that people can place on their desks or on the walls of their office.* Be aware however, many companies have invested a lot of money creating plaques, posters, and paperweights bearing the company's service policy only to find these items become little more than fancy office decorations. You must continually stress your customer service policy and remind people that your company takes it seriously.

- *Train everyone in the company on customer service skills, and make sure those skills are applied.* Never assume your staff automatically knows how to handle customers. Be sure they're trained on *internal* service excellence as well. There's no way external customers can be serviced well if your people are not servicing each other well.

- *Make it mandatory for managers to evaluate their people not only on the quality of their work, but on customer service.* If your people know they are being evaluated on their service performance, then it will become a priority to them.

- *Reward employees who demonstrate service excellence.* In doing so, you'll be sending a message to everyone about what you feel is important. When other employees see what gets rewarded in the company, then they, too, will display those behaviors.

- *What gets measured gets attention, so set up a system for customer service measurement.* Include customer retention rates, customer satisfaction, response times, and number of complaints. Determine what measures are important to your business and make your people accountable for improving them.

- *Set the example yourself and provide quality service to your employees by valuing them and treating them with dignity and respect.* I often wonder how companies can expect their employees to provide exceptional service if they're not being treated exceptionally well by their own management. Create an environment that attracts Achievers and encourages high performance using some of the methods in our next chapter.

Remember: Everyone in your organization must have *total dedication* to your customers. When they do, then you're in a better position to maintain strength in the marketplace and achieve superior performance and results. If your people don't know how to treat customers well, then your company will be a place where customers buy once. Just once.

Create a Loyalty Program

A customer loyalty program can be an effective method to retain customers and increase sales. A loyalty program is basically a marketing effort designed to reward customers who give you repeat business. If your program is interesting and creative, it can provide a strong reason for customers to stay with your company, purchase from your store or use your products and services instead of flocking to your competitor. It can also be an effective way to learn who your best customers are.

The success of a customer loyalty program depends upon several factors: the level of commitment your company has to implement it, whether or not it's simple to promote and easy to use, and the desirability of its rewards to your customer. All these must be considered before you embark on a customer loyalty program. Depending on your business, here are a few ideas you might consider if you want to establish a customer loyalty program:

- Mail a special membership or a customer card that entitles customers to "bonus points" based on the frequency or amount of purchases. The build up of these bonus points entitles customers to special discounts, free products, etc. You can mail customers regular statements showing available bonus points. Airlines, credit card companies, and retail establishments use programs like these. Innovative business-to-business companies often do it, as well.
- Contests also encourage repeat business. They're popular with the public, giving people the opportunity to win valuable prizes. Think of companies like McDonalds who give popular game pieces or toys with a purchase. Companies run contests where people find winning entries under bottle caps, beneath wrappers, behind labels and inside boxes. Of course, if you sell a service and not a product, you can still utilize contests to generate business. A contest on your web site is great, too! Be creative. Be different!
- A simple money-off coupon can be an effective way to reward repeat customers. People always enjoy buy-one-get-one-free deals, "20% off" coupons, or whatever special deal works for your business.

- A customer loyalty program that rewards customers who refer new business to you is always smart. The reward may be a gift, a gift certificate, merchandise they can select out of a catalog or a substantial discount on a product they regularly order. It should include a handwritten note or formal thank you letter. I've often heard people say that nothing turns them off more than lack of gratitude. In my opinion, referring business to someone who doesn't bother to thank the person in some way is highly unprofessional.

Reward

Another effective method of developing true loyalty is to offer rewards that provide an immediate benefit and do not involve any action on the part of the customer. One approach might be to offer an on-the-spot discount to a customer who has regularly given you business. There are not only no special requirements for this but also the fact that it was unexpected gives the discount extra value in the customer's eye.

Deliver

What happens when customers depend on you … and you deliver? They depend on you even more. Tell your people to under-promise and over-deliver. For example, if your customer wants the product delivered in two weeks and you know it will likely take three, say, "I'd like to be able to tell you it will be two weeks, but I want to be honest with you, it will take three. But I'll do everything I possibly can to get it to you sooner." Then try like heck to get it to them in their timeframe.

A woman in hotel sales once told me, "The hotel had to stop their promise of a free night's stay if anything went wrong because they couldn't keep their promise. There was always some small detail that was forgotten or a mistake made by the front desk, housekeeping, bell person, or room service staff." I also have a client in the banking industry that is still wondering why they ever promised cash for every mistake they made. Don't be like most politicians. Make sure your company can keep the promises it makes.

Remember, if customer loyalty programs work for the direct consumer market, business-to-business enterprises should consider employing a program that reflects their customer service philosophy: deeper discounts to long term customers, additional product features at no extra charge, free after-sales support, etc.

Customer loyalty is achieved by providing consistently good service and human interaction that demonstrates that your company cares about its customers. Customers need to be appreciated—very appreciated. What has your company done lately to show customers they appreciate them?

Establish and Build Strong Relationships

There's been much discussion about how development of personal relationships between company people and customers is lacking in today's increasingly automated world. With more sophisticated technological advances in communication, it will be even more important that every person who has customer contact makes every effort to nurture and develop a special closeness with customers.

Fix It Quick!

Correct mistakes quickly and smoothly. Errors, such as mistakes in billing, or putting the wrong information on an order, can happen. Rectify them with an apology and a graceful comment such as, "I'm so sorry this happened. Let's fix it immediately." Carry out remedial action promptly. No customer is happy when they lose time from your mistakes. If a problem arises or a mistake has been made, handling them the right way builds relationships and can be a strong factor in establishing loyalty.

Soften the Toughies!

One of the most challenging situations is to turn difficult customers into loyal customers. If you can do that, then you may not only gain a new loyal customer but also create an advocate for your business. When you encounter a difficult customer, instead of getting angry and defensive, be respectful, apologetic and humble.

An owner of a well-known fast-food franchise told me about a situation where a demanding customer implied that he'd been overcharged for his food. She knew the customer was mistaken but, instead of arguing, she apologized and told him she would not charge him for his lunch that day. She impressed the customer by listening to him and offering a solution that exceeded his expectations. Consequently, the gentleman became one of her most loyal customers. He introduced more people to her establishment and always complimented her on both her friendliness and the cleanliness of her store. (There's a lesson there!) He visited so frequently that he and the owner became good friends.

You can establish life-long friendships and build strong customer loyalty by going the extra mile and handling each customer with special care—whether they act like Dorothy or the Wicked Witch of the West.

Being extraordinarily responsive in your delivery of service to your customers is the mark of an Achiever. Moment-by-moment, I encourage you to strive for excellence in your delivery of service to both your external *and* internal customers. In doing so, you'll set an example for everyone in your company and help maintain the momentum needed to obtain customer loyalty. At the end of each day, you, your customers and your coworkers will be the final judges of your performance.

Chapter 11

Value Your People—Your Ultimate Competitive Advantage

With all the re-engineering, reorganizing, TQM, paradigm shifting, outsourcing, and all the other "surefire" methods out there to beat the competition, businesses must recognize that it's their human capital who hold the key to sustainable, long-term growth. They create the force that helps you beat the competition. Within them lie solutions to your problems, methods to improve productivity, creative ideas to improve products and service, and insight on what management needs to do to move forward. That assumes, of course, that you have the right people in your organization to come out on top. You need a workforce of people who come to work every day ready to serve customers.

One of the most challenging problems facing all businesses today is attracting and keeping Achievers—those skilled workers with desirable characteristics. If you're in a leadership position, you've probably been reading about them and wondering, "*Where* do I find these highly competent Achievers who love their job, have a sense of direction, are accountable, flexible and adaptable through change, have a positive attitude and all those other quality characteristics. And if I'm lucky enough to find them, how do I *keep* them?"

This chapter will provide executives, managers, supervisors and business owners with the answers to these questions, and offer important information on how to create an environment for high performance.

Today, businesses must sell themselves to talented people. The trend has shifted from what a job candidate can offer a company to what the company can offer the candidate. The Achievers they want to hire and hold onto are difficult to retain because today, they can work almost anywhere they choose. This is especially true for today's "knowledge" workers who recognize that the cards are now in the hands of the job candidates. Take a look at Cisco's Website (www.cisco.com) and the "Make Friends @ Cisco" program. They have fashioned a highly innovative recruiting process in order to attract quality employees.

An enlightened organization cares about its people, treats them with respect, provides quality training and development, and values them as much as they value their customers. It makes sense that people who feel truly valued will demonstrate the same to customers. Under these conditions, everyone wins! Most importantly, the company develops a *reputation* for doing so and may now be considered as "Employers of Choice."

However, this should not be considered as an exclusive club reserved for large corporations. Even if you're a small organization with only a handful of employees, you can strive to be considered an Employer of Choice within your field as long as you have a similar culture. It's this type of environment that attracts and retains Achievers who are dedicated, effective and perform well. The definition is: Any employer of any size in the public, private, or not-for-profit sector that attracts, optimizes, and holds top talent for long tenure because the employees choose to be there.

Whether they're seeking a management or support position in your company, if you ask Achievers what they would look for in a job, they would likely say, "I want an interesting and challenging job with a company that has a great future. I want to work for one that's well managed and has a culture that demonstrates they value their people. I want to be recognized, appreciated and rewarded for my work. I want a great boss who will give me a voice in the decision-making, and work where supportive people who have a good sense of humor surround me. And, it would be nice to have a little fun once in a while. In simple terms, I want to work at a place where I like to show up every day." This seems like a lot to ask for, so let's look at these one at a time.

- **I want an interesting and challenging job**

   Whether they fall into the Slacker, Coaster or Achiever categories, everyone would like a job they find interesting. You can count on the Slackers to complain no matter how interesting their job may be. The Coasters will need strong leadership and involvement to keep them interested.

The Achievers absolutely require interesting work if you want them to stay with your organization. It's the challenging part of the job that separates them from their brethren. They're attracted to and will likely stay in environments where they have an opportunity to express and challenge themselves. They thrive on a great deal of creative freedom where they can take some risks without fear of being reprimanded for failure.

• I want to work for a company with a great future

All employees have a right to know where the company is headed. Effectively communicate your company's direction with clarity and consistency, and involve your employees in helping define that direction. Just like people, companies can also be Slackers, Coasters, and Achievers. A company that doesn't have a strong focus on its future and is content to maintain its current levels of sales and profits is little more than a Coaster, and an ambitious employee will not be satisfied to stay with such an organization.

• I want to work for a company that's well-managed

Achievers recognize the importance of management's performance. Many organizations have failed because its management was not in touch with the reality of the perceptions, opinions, expectations, needs and problems of their people. Achievers become discouraged when their leaders are not performing. Perhaps the sales reps aren't getting the help they need, the warehouse is in a mess or their branch isn't delivering the level of service the company expects of them. In these circumstances, the boss is the one who is the Slacker!

If the management of your company cannot effectively lead, nothing else matters. If you're in a position to make leadership changes in your organization, then do something about it. We need fewer bosses and more leaders who will work to establish an atmosphere that supports highly motivated, creative and solution-focused people who serve both customers and each other well.

• I want to work for a company that has strong values

Achievers will gravitate toward a company that espouses values in sync with their own. While the work and pay are important components to attracting workers, don't underestimate the importance of values.

A company can promote many different values. Below are several values that, in my opinion, an Achiever would want:

- An environment of *trust* is important to Achievers. They need to feel they can trust management and their coworkers, and that the communication they receive from management is completely honest.

- Business *integrity* is another important value. Employees need to be able to trust that the company will act legally and ethically in its business dealings. No one likes hearing about a scandal on the evening news.

- *Safety* must be a strong value. Companies must do all they can to protect its workers from unsafe working conditions and enforce safety standards.

- Another important value is the recognition of an employee's *personal life*. All companies want their employees to maintain a high level of productivity; thus, methods to help in this area have become increasingly important in today's workplace. Employees want their company to recognize their lives extend beyond the company walls. Companies that promote work/family balance will have more productive employees in the long run. Exercise rooms and day-care services are also desirable. Many organizations are also including a paternity leave in their benefits package.

- *Health* and *wellness* is highly important to Achievers. This involves everything from providing adequate health care benefits to having healthy foods in the employee cafeteria. Not every company has the resources to provide an on-site health care facility, but providing access to wellness resources are of great benefit to their people.

- Achievers enjoy working for companies who are *community-focused*. They respect an employer that donates money to local charities, regularly sponsors or participates in community events and seeks opportunities to be of service to others. Furthermore, employees expect a company to do its part to protect the environment.

- Finally, *education* is an important value to Achievers. They not only want be trained in new skills but expect the company to provide ongoing training and development.

- **I want to work for a company with a good culture**

An organization's culture is the result of their upper level executives' attitudes, philosophy, values and opinions. If your organization's culture is suffering, you must first look at management for the cause. If you have a positive culture, the same holds true. The best leaders create the type of culture where teamwork is encouraged and people work together for the common good of the organization. The culture should foster open communication, respect for others, and require integrity in all business dealings. It should encourage people to perform at exceptional levels but make certain they're supported well by management. People can become discouraged when performance expectations are high but the company does nothing to help them attain their goals.

- **I want to be recognized, appreciated and rewarded for my work**

As Dale Carnegie said, "All human beings wear two invisible signs. One says, 'Make me feel important.' The other says, 'Appreciate me.' "

People need respect and approval, and to feel a sense of accomplishment. They want to be rewarded for good performance as often and as soon as possible. Great leaders say, "Thank you" often. They appreciate their people and their people know it. Not only do you want to reward employees when they provide exceptional quality service or meet sales objectives, but also to reward them for the small things that make a difference. When you do so, it will improve overall employee performance. Remember to not only reward individuals but also more often, reward team accomplishments.

- **I want a great boss**

There should be a "Zero-Tolerance for Bad Bosses" rule in your company. Based on my experience working with hundreds of companies, I have found the Number One cause of job dissatisfaction in America is working for a bad boss. If you have a problem with employee morale, the first area to examine is the company's leadership. Poor leaders can pass their weaknesses to others. They can let their ego or need for power and control get in the way of doing what's best. They may dwell on a mistake rather than discuss how to prevent it from recurring.

Poor leaders tend to create more Coasters by breaking down high-performers. They may have been Achievers when they were hired, but a bad boss all too often erodes their attitude and performance level, holds them back, or shoots down their ideas. Perhaps a destructive leader gave them "lip-service," reprimanded them in front of others or micromanaged their projects. Their boss may have showed favoritism, took credit for their ideas, or permitted Slackers to get away with negative behavior, thus pulling them down to become Coasters who feel that no matter what they say or do, they will never make an impact.

Great leaders hire the best people and let them run with the ball. They don't micromanage. They know that giving people the responsibility and authority to accomplish the results they expect is one of the strongest ways they can show they appreciate and respect their abilities. They not only know what characteristics to look for when hiring people, but they know where else to "find" Achievers.

Great leaders can turn Coasters into Achievers by encouraging them, believing in them, developing and coaching them. They know that if they work to build their subordinates' self-esteem and bring out the best in them, they can make new people out of them. They know how to unlock their employees' full talents and put those talents to work. Their mission is to help every worker attain his or her full potential as an employee and as a human being so he or she can perform in today's increasingly competitive and challenging environment.

Think back to your school days. Did you not have certain teachers for whom you would walk through fire because they brought out the best in you? Did you not have someone who believed in you before you believed in yourself? As simple as it sounds, a great leader is simply a great human being who inspires others. If you're liked, respected and trusted, your people will give you their best efforts.

The key to employee motivation and retaining Achievers is to motivate them from within. In order to do that, you must do what I told Dan, the new sales manager, "Make people feel they're working *with* you, not *for* you." If your people are feeling they are working *for* you, then you're creating *robots*—people who simply go through the motions and do what they're told. Robots will not come forward with their ideas because they do what you tell them to do.

They only follow orders. They will exhibit no initiative and will never take ownership for the company's success. If they feel they are working *for* you, you'll never inspire them to be creative and innovative.

Make people feel they're working *with* you with an open environment. This is always better than an authoritarian style as in that type of atmosphere, employees are afraid to say anything. In the past, many organizations were run like dictatorships where people were afraid to step over the line or make suggestions. Motivating through fear may have worked in the past, but now it's considered downright rotten. People need to work in a positive atmosphere where they are void of any fear of pointing out problems and suggesting new ways to serve customers and improve productivity.

Once during a leadership program, an executive challenged me with, "I don't have time for these Motherhood issues." I explained to him, "You don't need to look upon this as an enormous task. You don't need to have long meaningful discussions and spend lots of time with each person. Your people don't need a long speech. You must simply be a 'straight shooter.' Speak what's on your mind and be consistent and direct. When you see them doing something good, tell them. That also holds true if you need to criticize them. People need frequent baseline communication about their performance and expect feedback from their leaders."

- **I want to have a voice in the decision-making**

Achievers are attracted to organizations that have a high level of employee involvement, where they can participate in idea-sharing and problem-solving sessions like those we discussed in our chapter on creativity. Establish self-directed teams or task forces to help in this area. Don't make the mistake of asking only your Achievers to partake in these sessions. All your people need to feel they play a vital role in your organization and should also have a voice in the decision-making process.

One of my clients, a CEO in the telecommunications industry, uses an interesting technique for idea-sharing. He has each of his executives practice hands-on role reversal with three different employees once a month for structured discussions. Here are their ground rules: (1) They must leave their titles at the door; (2) The executives must ask questions and listen; (3) Employees must be open and assertive in their discussions.

The reason for the success of this practice is that it's ongoing and not a one-shot deal. It also stimulates employees to continuously generate more and better ideas and creates an understanding of each other's pressures.

When employees offer suggestions and recommendations for solutions, the company needs to make sure they *act* on those ideas. It would be insincere to ask employees to participate in decision-making and then ignore their input. If you determine that you simply cannot act upon employees' suggestions, then honestly explain why. Whenever possible, find parts of their solutions that are viable or elements that can be implemented in the future. Be sure to praise your people for any ideas they offer to keep them creatively charged. They need to know their efforts are appreciated.

- **I want to be surrounded by *supportive* people who have a good sense of humor**

    Achievers will quickly become Coasters if they're not fully supported by their coworkers. That's why those negative Slackers who pull everyone down with them must be confronted, as they'll never support anyone unless they're forced to. I have rarely delivered a program where people don't come up to me afterwards and complain about the Slackers who work beside them.

    All too often, these Slackers should never have been hired in the first place. Perhaps they interviewed well or fudged on their job application. When people are hired, they must receive a clear indication of what is expected of them regarding not only their performance but also their attitude. I recommend you establish a "Zero Tolerance for Negativity" culture, and when you hire people, make certain they receive that message loud and clear during the initial interview in a tactful manner. Let them know your culture values providing quality *internal* customer service just as much as it values providing quality service externally. Let them know you also encourage humor in the workplace to ease any tension that may occur on any given day.

    What do we do with the Slackers? If we could simply fire them our lives would be easier, but that's not so easy. Besides, maybe there's a reason for their behavior. Confront them and tactfully explain how their attitude negatively affects others. (See the chapter "Find Beauty in the Beast—Dealing With Difficult People.")

If they have performed well in the past and are now performing poorly, ask them if there is anything occurring externally that has caused this. Perhaps they're experiencing conflict in their department or are having personal problems. Ask them what you can do to help.

After you try to resolve the issue, watch for improvements in their performance. If you do not see any, you must confront them a second time. If you must confront them a third time, then you must inform that them that if their performance does not improve, you'll have to take stronger measures. Of course, the actions you may be allowed to take might be dictated by personnel policies, union agreements, etc., but the bottom line is that you must not ignore people who do not help support a positive work environment.

If we lived in a perfect world, our workforce would consist largely of Achievers, but that's not reality. The majority of our workforce consists of Coasters, which is why you must rally the Achievers around you and ask them to support and encourage the Coasters and help bring out the best in them. Provide your people with training in teamwork so they can experience being stronger as a team than they are on their own. They'll also learn to communicate with each other more effectively so that they can understand each other's pressures, workload, and deadlines.

- **I want to work where I can look forward to showing up every day and maybe even have some fun**

    Fun in the workplace. What a novel idea! Most people think that we need to take our work seriously. Of course we do, but that doesn't mean that we can't have a little fun along the way. Encourage your people to use a little creativity to come up with ideas to keep the workplace interesting and fun. Do something spontaneous and out of the ordinary. Below are a few methods I've heard about from my clients:
    - Try adding a little humor in the workplace by posting funny jokes on the office message board. (Keep it clean!)
    - Celebrate birthdays, anniversaries and other special occasions. Take the honoree out to lunch, bring in a cake, blow up balloons or bring in a magician!
    - Set up barbecue grills in the parking lot and have a cookout.

- Take photographs of people and display them with your own funny captions.
- Create contests for every possible thing you can think of: sales, best customer service, person most responsible for maintaining high morale in their department, best idea of the month, best attendance record, neatest desk, etc.
- Provide training programs that are energizing and fun!
- When someone has had a really rough day, leave a funny card on his or her desk. Have a few handy in your desk so you can be spontaneous.
- Don't forget the issue of life-balance. Encourage sports teams and consider including spouses and children.
- Follow the example of Dave Duffield of PeopleSoft. When CNN featured him a business program, he emphasized how he concerns himself only with business behavior and not politics. He related how he sustains an upbeat atmosphere. He has a "Jumping for Joy" club. His people play air hockey to relieve stress during lunch or before and after work. Barbecues in the parking lot occur often and he provides free bagels on Friday. He makes sure the restrooms are always clean. When it comes to taking a donut, or using an envelope or stamp, everything is "on your honor." There is a large mural of his employees on the wall in the reception area. He also has an "Adopt a Pet" program." Once a week he brings in a stray pet from the local animal shelter for adoption. (Many shelters will be eager to bring out a selection of pets to your company.) I admire Mr. Duffield a great deal.

If you would like more ideas on how to regenerate spirit in the workplace, you can find them in *"CARE Packages for the Workplace,"* by Barbara A. Glanz, ISBN 0-07-024267-4. It provides dozens of specific "how-to" ideas that anyone can apply in their job to make a difference.

Demonstrate your own values and value your people. If you focus on their health, morale and productivity, they will perform well. Unlock their potential and make sure they're "in tune" with your business strategy. Show them you care about them as much as you care about your customers and involve them in the decision-making process. Don't forget to let them have the most fun they possibly can as long as they maintain their professionalism. When you create this type of high performance workplace and can offer all an Achiever would look for in a job, you will not only be able to hire, create and retain Achievers but will be amazed at how they will help your company to compete and win.

Chapter 12

Leading Through Change

One of the most challenging and important responsibilities of a leader is not only to create an environment for high performance, but also to institute any major change as smoothly as possible. If change is not managed correctly disgruntled employees, turnover, and poor performance and even chaos can be the result. Here are effective methods to help your people manage the transition process.

Communicate the Reason for Change, the Direction and Goals

Be sure everyone in the organization understands the vision of where the company is going and why. Make them a part of the plan so that they assume ownership. You need to explain to people that the changes you're asking them to go through are necessary in order for the organization to remain competitive and to continue to grow.

Communicate management goals and direction to every level of the company: "With this acquisition, I know our product line has doubled in size, but we need to double the overall number of accounts with the new combined product line. I know things are very different from what you're used to, but we're committed to helping everyone adjust to the changes. It will take time to get everyone up to speed, but I'm counting on you to make it happen. And when we do, we'll be the Number One Company in the industry."

Establish an Atmosphere of Open Communication

Open communication is important in every organization at all times, but it becomes even more critical during times of change. As you plan the changes you wish to make, consider developing a concurrent communication strategy to remind people what the changes are, what the expectations are, and the progress you're making in your change efforts.

In a changing environment, people lose their motivation if they're not kept informed about what's going on around them. The less informed they are, the more likely it will have a negative impact on their performance. Your silence may be interpreted as insensitivity, or may even make people believe that the results expected from the change are not as effective as you thought they might be. With open communication, you help build trust between yourself and your people. Communicate what you know and, as uncomfortable as it sounds, communicate what you don't know about the future. Failing to address the difficult questions—questions people may already be asking each other and their peers—does not make the issues go away. For example, if you're not sure you'll be able to retain every employee if sales don't increase by 15 percent, say so. They'll respect you for your honesty.

Introduce Change Gradually Whenever Possible

Too much change at once can create chaos for yourself and your organization. You may feel your people are ready to respond to change, but they may not be able to absorb the changes as quickly as you like. Assimilating new information and learning new systems or procedures takes time. Give your people time to understand the changes before introducing more. This is my opinion. However, some managers have told me they prefer a single big macro change rather than several small ones. They feel if everyone learns the game plan all at once, then it's over and they can get on with it. They contend that disruption continues during the change process whether it's a big one or small ones dragged out over time. You know your people, so think about what would be best for them.

If you're leading through the midst of change, remember that *you* may be committed to it but others may not have had time to accept the changes, let alone understand them. For instance, let's say you own a small consulting firm where the employees have historically worked out of your office. Moving forward, you recognize that employees will need to begin working for extensive periods of time at client locations, sometimes even out of town. This will mean a big culture change for the small but tight-knit group of consultants who work for you. You'll have to make sure they understand the need for the change and help introduce it incrementally, if possible. Perhaps you can begin by having consultants work on client locations a week or so at a time and gradually extend that time to longer visits. You may want to make sure that you plan "staff days" or social outings so that the consultants have the opportunity to maintain their sense of camaraderie.

Perhaps you have traditionally sold your product or service through partnerships and now the company has restructured and is selling directly to the end user. You'll need to meet with your sales force so they can share their best ideas on how to find qualified prospects.

Remember it's important to move at a pace that will ensure you meet your business goals while giving your people the opportunity to process the changes for themselves.

Ask for Accountability

Ask your people to be accountable to each other for maintaining high morale. By placing an equal value on teamwork, professional behavior, sales performance, and accountability, you and your peers will be able to provide better service to both customers and to each other. Even if change is difficult and may need to be introduced incrementally, people still need to be held responsible for making the required changes. Reward those who have made the transition and are now working the way you expect them to behave in the new environment. For instance, if you have decided that cross-functional teamwork is important, then acknowledge the successes of those who have successfully completed projects through teamwork. Soon, those who are not working as team players will get the message.

Be in Tune to Difficulties Some May Be Experiencing

Recognize that most people fear change but it affects each one differently. Some will be more adaptable than others will. Many Achievers may enjoy being stretched beyond their present comfort zone, but others may be completely overwhelmed and will wonder if they will be able to keep their job. You need to let them know you understand the challenges they're facing and your job as their manager is to help them through it. Make sure you provide adequate training in new products or procedures, and keep your door open so people can come in to discuss any apprehension.

You want to provide a comfortable environment where people can air their concerns. It's normal for people to resist change, so the more patience you show the sooner they will adapt.

Encourage Acceptance and Focus on Positive Opportunities

When people complain about a new system, process, or procedure, you need to acknowledge the difficulty and explain that once they're comfortable with it, their work will become easier and success will benefit everyone.

Communicate to your people they have a choice. They can be either an advocate or a resistor to change, but if everyone does their part, together, they can accomplish the goals. Help them to see that negativity will only hold everyone back and customer service will be affected. Encourage support, and make them feel a sense of excitement about themselves and the company as you grow together.

Ask for Input ... Give Feedback ... Take Action!

Employee involvement is the key to creating high performance through the midst of change. As I said in the previous chapter, ask your people for their ideas on how you can support each other. This is especially important when in the midst of change. Ask them how you can help each other to ease the transition process. Many companies are guilty of under-using the ideas and suggestions of their people when going through change, and do not take full advantage of their knowledge and experience. If employees are not involved, they won't feel that they're part of the change; they'll feel more like victims of it!

Ask how your people are doing. Listen, and encourage cooperation and honesty. Talk to that person who is coming to work with a chip on his shoulder. Ask what you can do to help. Encourage upward feedback from everyone on his or her attitudes, concerns, issues and frustrations that are related to the change.

Be a Role Model

It's up to management to maintain employee morale through change. Set the tone; be a role model and be an example for others to follow. Let your team know that you're there to help them through it. Be accountable for the attitude that *you* bring to your job each day.

Encourage People to Be Solution-Focused, Not Problem-focused.

"For every problem there is a solution," should be a motto in your company. As problems occur during change, the Slackers and Coasters will most likely wait for management to fix them. At the onset of change, let your people know they're expected to help identify problems and focus on offering solutions. Changes rarely occur without glitches, so ask them to brainstorm ways to solve the problems.

Take Time to Train

To thwart loss of productivity during change, you need to make sure your people have the necessary skills to succeed. Training must be seen as a top priority. The time you invest in training will eventually pay off in increased profits and service quality. As you look at the changes you plan to implement, you should ask yourself these training-related questions:

- What is the needed level of competence to support the change?
- What training will be needed to bring them up to that level of competence?
- During the time needed for training, how will they maintain their current workload?

Don't treat training like getting a cold—if they hang around long enough, maybe they'll catch it. Training helps to alleviate the stress common during change. It demonstrates you do appreciate their efforts and are willing to help them along.

Alleviate Job Pressure

Meeting the demands placed upon people during change requires managing job pressure for you and others. Laugh a little! Change may be serious, but people who have fun at work are more productive and less anxious during change. Encourage the type of upbeat and fun atmosphere we discussed earlier.

You've heard the old adage: "The only constant is change." Yes, change is inevitable, but it doesn't have to be agonizing. If you make a conscious effort to help your people through change and implement strategies to ease the transition, you can build a winning team ... and after you've helped them through the current change, then you'll be ready to help them through the next one.

Section 3

Talk Your Way
to the Top

I have asked the following question to numerous groups in a wide variety of industries, and have always received the same answer: "What, in your opinion, is the Number One skill people need to achieve success in today's competitive world—no matter what they do for a living?"

The answer? *Communication skills.* No matter what you do, if you're unable to think on your feet, "talk smart," to present your ideas to others, and deal with all types of people, it will hold you back from winning.

As I said earlier, I fully realize that many parts of this book could have been extended into an entire book in itself. This section is one of them. In fact, several of my peers who were kind enough to read my manuscript before it went to print advised me not to even include this section but save it for a future book. I asked myself how I could possibly write a book on how to beat the competition if I don't provide my readers with *people skills*. Since you're reading this, I did what my gut told me to do. I hope you memorize some of its content, because this stuff works!

Chapter 13

The Art of Influencing People

S tudies reveal that 85 percent of your career success is in direct proportion to your ability to communicate. However, I believe that 85 percent of your overall success in *life* is in direct proportion to your ability to communicate your wants, needs and ideas to others. In the business world specifically, you need to be able to influence people, whether your goal is to increase sales, improve management/employee relationships, implement change, build customer relationships, create a winning team, convey the value of your product to customers, gain support, or all of these.

The ability to influence people may seem elusive to you but some people seem to be born with it. They can convince a customer to buy a new product, get their idle coworker to put in extra effort or persuade their boss to pursue a new business strategy. Other people seem to struggle just to get people to comply with their simple requests. (Some would be thrilled if they could just convince their teenager to turn down their blasting music!) No one is born with this talent. To some people influencing others comes more naturally, but it's as much a learned skill as it is an innate ability.

As a child, I was shy and introverted. My two older sisters were also timid. The reason we were all quiet and reserved is due to the environment in which we were raised. Our parents felt that children should be seen and not heard—-a very rare cultural trait for Italians! At the same time, since the age of eight, I always dreamed of a career in the performing arts. My mother supported my aspiration and kept telling me that I was going to "get discovered," that someone was just going to come up to this shy child, recognize her talent and take her to the top. She was so wrong! I realized that if I wanted to get anywhere in this world, I would have to be less introverted and become more confident. So, as I worked on my musical skills, I also worked on my ability to interact with people and build rapport with others because, as an entertainer, being able to connect with audiences is crucial.

Just as I'd learned the right notes to play on the violin, or where to place a high note when singing, when I shifted my career to the business world, I had to learn the right words to say, how to say them, and when to say them. Most importantly, I had to practice them repeatedly to make them perfect—as a musician would—until they became a habit. Just as I did (if I could do it, so can you!), you can improve your influencing skills if you learn to use the right language and memorize effective key phrases to apply in various circumstances. You'll also need to learn how to read and respond to people, and how to ask for what you want! These are all things that we will address in this chapter.

Take Charge

Influencing people comes easier to those who are more assertive than others. Not to be confused with aggressive people, assertive people have a depth of understanding about themselves and others. They know what they want and how they feel. Most importantly, they know how to *communicate* those feelings to others. They are usually both physically and mentally healthy because they can express themselves, rarely keeping things inside.

As you seek to influence others, you must first look hard and deep at yourself, and see yourself as others see you. As you examine the image you project, keep in mind that you influence others in three areas:

- Who you are.
- What they hear from you.
- What they see you do or not do.

Let's begin with who you are.

Who Are You?

You need to have a strong sense of self and to recognize the kind of person you are. Are you a strong leader who's not afraid to take charge? Are you a caring person? Are you someone who's willing to help? Do you have strong values? Are you a person who strives to please your customers? Do you love your job and treat people well?

Estelle, a manager of an upscale hotel, is well respected by both her employees and her customers. If a problem occurs during a major conference, she handles the matter personally. She doesn't delegate the problem to an assistant, even if it means taking off her pumps and climbing a ladder to change a light bulb. When she sees that the receptionists at the desk are busy, she jumps right in and assists with hotel check-ins and check-outs. She helps everyone, from her district manager putting together a local marketing strategy to the room service attendant delivering a late-night snack. She puts in long hours, not because she has too much work to complete but because she clearly loves what she does. She always has a ready compliment for the maids, the bellhops, the concierge and the maintenance crew. Because Estelle is perceived as a thoughtful, sincere, and enthusiastic leader, she never faces resistance when she needs to persuade her subordinates.

What Are Others Hearing You Say?

You can influence others if you're an "encourager." You want to make people feel good about themselves, and speak in terms of positive outcomes. Do they hear empathy and caring? Do they hear a tone of voice that sounds genuine and sincere? Do they hear "thanks" and "I appreciate you" often? Do they hear words that encourage people and bring out the best in them? Do they hear positive reinforcement? Do they hear an open-minded response when they make suggestions, share ideas or give their opinions? Do they hear a person who listens but doesn't talk? Does what they consistently hear let them know where you stand? Do they hear assertive communication with tact and diplomacy when necessary? Do you sound confident and knowledgeable? Do you sound enthusiastic without sounding overly excited? Or do they hear someone who vacillates back and forth on what they want to do and why?

Ted is an anomaly. As a project manager in a retail sales environment, he works with a lot of "Type A" sales people who typically move, speak, and react at a frenetic pace. Ted, though, is much more deliberate and subdued. He doesn't have the kind of voice that excites people, but when he communicates, he makes it clear that he understands the person's deadlines and pressures. He listens to their suggestions, but is not afraid to respectfully disagree when warranted. He knows how to manage projects effectively and, therefore, projects a low-key confidence in his voice.

Like Estelle, Ted also has a strong ability to influence others and has an excellent relationship with the sales managers he supports. They hear Ted's calm and empathetic voice and respond accordingly.

Don't Tell Them ... Show Them

What do they see? You want to make sure your actions are consistent with the values and traits to which you aspire. Do you project professionalism? Do others see someone who "leads by example?" Do they see someone who rolls up her sleeves, moves people and gets the job done? Do they see non-verbal communication that has a positive message? Do they see actions that demonstrate that you do what you say you'll do? Do they see consistent demonstrations of your values? Do they see someone with a positive attitude? Do they see someone who appears credible in the eyes of others? Do they see competency? Do they see someone who is willing to do what they are asking others to do? Do they see that you do what you say you'll do? Is your word your bond?

Sandra owns her own advertising agency and is well respected by her clients and employees. At work, she stresses teamwork, and it's not uncommon for her to get in early to help the graphic designers prepare their storyboards, and stay late with the writers to help them proof ad copy. Her clients are impressed with her understanding of market share, competitor analysis, and product placement. When a client shares an idea for an advertisement, Sandra's eyes light up and a broad smile spreads across her face. As a result, she can easily convince clients to take a gamble with her marketing campaigns, and then assemble an enthusiastic staff ready to work hard for her to create stellar results.

Estelle, Ted, and Sandra remind us that the image we convey to others is the first step in learning how to influence others. People are always looking at the kind of person you are—not only what you say but also what you do.

It would be easy to influence others if we only had to worry about our own image. In order to successfully persuade others to your point of view and to get them to do the things you want, you need to be aware of several factors about the other person that affect your ability to exercise influence.

1. Size Up

First, you must know how to tailor your conversations to the personality of each person with whom you interact. Each of us is unique and, consequently, we respond differently to persuasion. Some people feel easily threatened; others seem oblivious to subtle persuasion. Some folks naturally trust other people while others are skeptical. Some people are warm and congenial; others are negative and sometimes even despondent. You need to vary your approach to each person. Later in this chapter, as you read the various techniques of influence, keep in mind the personalities of those with whom you spend most of your time.

2. Access the Agenda

Seek to understand the personal and professional agendas of those with whom you work—you have *your* objective, but what's *their* agenda? Does it conflict with yours? Is it compatible? Is it completely different? You need to discover their WIIFM (What's In It For Me?) analysis and speak from there. Let's say you need a colleague's help on a project, but she's more concerned with making herself look good to your boss than in helping you succeed. If you're trying to convince her to assist you, you might speak less to how it would help you out while you're in a pinch and more to how the boss likes people who step up and help others on the team. In assessing another's agenda, learn to put yourself in another's position to ascertain their goals, dreams and desires. Then, shape your communication accordingly.

3. Attitude Again!

Determine the overriding attitudes of each person you work with most frequently. What are their beliefs and attitudes as they relate to what you want to accomplish? Do they value hard work?

Do they value their personal life? Are they hardheaded? Do they practice integrity? Or, do they have a win-at-all-cost attitude? When you understand other's attitudes, you'll see more clearly how they will view your position.

4. What's Happening?

What's their current state of mind? In other words, is anything happening in their situation that affects their current perception? For example, if you're speaking with a customer who just received a late shipment , maybe now isn't the time to persuade them to increase their order. If you're speaking to a group of managers who had to make drastic budget cuts, you may need to speak more in-depth about the cost-benefit of your proposal. Or if you're speaking to someone who's just lost a loved one, learn what you can about the circumstances so that you can adjust your approach as necessary.

5. He Said, She Said

How can you more effectively communicate, given gender differences? Men and women react differently. For example, men may be less likely to ask for help from a woman. (Nor will they ask for directions!) If you're a woman supervising a group of mostly men, you may need to take them into a relaxed atmosphere to get them to open up. You may have difficulty in finding the right approach to deliver necessary criticism or offer advice. If you're a man supervising a group of women, you'll need to be sure you don't come across as domineering or insensitive. Women tend to be more emotional than men are.

Take the time to observe the subtle differences between the way men and women communicate in your workplace. If you're in sales, be sure to shake a woman's hand when greeting her, just as you would a man's, and speak to her on equal ground.

6. Culture Check

Take a look at cultural differences. They also influence an individual's behavior. In some cultures, personal recognition is considered embarrassing. In other cultures, it's considered rude to discuss business without first getting to know the other party. Still other cultures frown on loud, boisterous appeals, while others expect it. If you know you'll be interacting with those from a culture different from your own, make sure you learn more about their background.

The bottom line to successfully influencing people lies not just in understanding what you want from the other person, but also in observing the factors listed above that result in their unique point of view. As a result of your closer observation, you'll gain new insights into how to more quickly gain support for your ideas.

Know Why!

Now that you're aware of how others perceive you and you know that each individual possesses unique factors that affect your influencing ability, another element to successfully influencing others is knowing the value or the benefits of the ideas and proposals you're suggesting. You should be able to articulate those benefits in order to convince the other person to accept, or at least take an interest in, your point of view. As we asked earlier, why should people do business with you, buy your product and do business with your company? Why should they join your association? Why should they be on a task force? Why should they provide quality customer service? If you can convince others of the value of your idea, suggestion or proposal, the easier it will be to get them to change their behavior … and that's really what influencing people is all about. Convincing others to accept your suggestion means that you're asking them to do something different or better.

Of course, you not only need to be able to share the benefits of your ideas and propositions, but you must also feel those benefits in your heart so as to make the other person feel what you feel. Successful sales people will tell you that it's not enough to just present a litany of features and benefits of a product or service, you need to be earnest about them. "Ours is the best engineering design," "We have the best after-hours service," "Our clients tell us we have the quickest delivery in the industry," "I know we have the best team in the field," and so on. The excitement of your project will be contagious, and if you're sincere, the other party will be convinced of your viewpoint.

Now that we've looked at the internal and external factors for influencing others, as well as the importance of knowing and believing the benefits of your ideas, let's look at specific techniques you can use to improve your ability to influence others.

Be Direct

The direct approach is often the most effective way to get your point across or bring an important matter to someone's attention. It's also respectful of other people's time. A good way to do this would be to say, "Hi Marie. I know how busy you are so I'll be brief. I need to let our new-hires know when they'll get the promotions they were promised. Every one of them has asked me when they'll take place."

Or, "Joe, we have a serious matter to discuss. Our general manager is not performing. The Board wants us to replace him."

Talk Smart

I call the ability to choose the right words in a given situation "Talking Smart." You may have a good idea for another person, but if the language you use turns that person off, then your ideas will not be well received. I'm reminded of a gentleman I know who serves on the board of a public library. He speaks with such arrogance and pomposity that none of his fellow board members will consider any of his ideas. This is unfortunate because on occasion he has come up with a few good arguments.

You'll find it easier to influence others if you can memorize a few simple words and phrases that will make a positive impact. Also, you can help your case by knowing which words and phrases to avoid—better yet, eliminating them from your vocabulary. Let's first look at the positive expressions and a few examples for each. As you review them, think of the situations where you might apply them.

Good Speaking Habits

"It's been my experience that ..."

"It's been my experience that whenever we hire people with no experience, our customers lose confidence in our ability to provide quality service." "It's been my experience that people who buy an automobile from our dealership will buy their next one from us as well." "It's been my experience that a one-shot training program doesn't work. We need to provide ongoing training for our people."

"I believe ..."

"I believe in your ability to operate that equipment," "I believe your approach to persuading the client is a good one," "I believe you're going to be delighted with our proposal," or "I believe your customers are going to be highly satisfied with our product."

"Our customers tell us ..."

"Our customers tell us this is the best method they have ever used," "Our customers tell us we have the best software to manage systems in our industry," "Our customers tell us their productivity has increased dramatically in their manufacturing operation," or "Our customers tell us they love ordering on our web site because it's so easy."

"Thanks so much for ..."

"Thanks so much for meeting with me today. I know you're busy, so I won't take up much of your time," "Thanks so much for sending that package out for me. It helped me out immensely." "Thanks so much for agreeing to talk to us about bidding on your project."(These should be the first words you say if you are meeting with a client.)

"I'm confident that ..."

"I'm confident that you'll find our proposal covers all the criteria you laid out." "I'm confident that our new sales strategy will increase revenues by 15%." "I'm confident we can help reduce your turnover." "I'm confident we can deliver exactly what you need." "I'm confident we can ship your order this week."

"I appreciate ..."

"I appreciate how quickly you responded." "I appreciate the difficult position your company is facing." "I appreciate how you handled that difficult client." "I appreciate how you kept your team focused." "I appreciate how hard you all worked to complete this project."

"Take a look and see for yourself ..."

"This printer makes the clearest copies in the industry. Take a look and see for yourself. The number of customer complaints has decreased dramatically." "Take a look and see for yourself, our architectural design is superb." "Take a look at these figures and see for yourself." "Take a look at this machine and see for yourself how quickly it runs."

"I enjoy ..."

"I enjoy working with you on this project." "I enjoy attending your customer focus group session." "I've enjoyed this conference." "I always enjoy talking with you." "I enjoy working with you."

"I liked the way you ..."

"I really liked the way you explained our return policy to that customer." "I really liked the way you reorganized the filing system." "I liked the way you handled the workers on the construction site." "I liked the way you stepped up to the plate and voiced your opinion." "I like your suggestion for eliminating overtime."

"What can I do to help?"

"It looks as if you still have a lot to do before you leave today. What can I do to help?" "Are you ready for tomorrow's meeting? What can I do to help?" "You seem to be having difficulty managing the new-hires. What I can I do to help?"

"Would you be good enough to ...? Would you be so kind ... ?"

"Would you be good enough to give me a hand with these cost projections?" "Would you be nice enough to help me find out who I would speak to about this in your company?" "Would you be good enough to put this on Mr. Smith's desk, and let me know what he thinks about our proposal." "Would you be so kind as to send a second copy of your report to the vice-president?" "Would you be so kind as to help Corey reconcile the month-end reports?"

"That's a good idea / point / observation."

"That's a good point. I didn't know that we couldn't buy that component for less than $500." "Delegating the task to the new accountant! Great idea!" "That's a good idea the task force suggested."

"Thank you!"

"Thank you" is the most important phrase in your business and personal life. Say it often.

Bad Speaking Habits

Just as there are phrases that will help you influence people, there are also phrases that can make influencing people more difficult for you, not to mention that you may come across as sounding weak.

"To tell you the truth ..."

"To tell you the truth, our product is simply the best in the marketplace." "To tell you the truth, I believe you'll benefit from our services."

"To be honest ..."

"To be honest, I can give you the best deal." "To be honest, I have sold hundreds of this product."

"To be frank ..."

"To be frank, I don't think this will go over." "To be frank, you should have done more."

"You have to ..." / "You'd better ..." / "You must ..."

"You have to do this if you expect us to honor your service request." "You have to stand in line" "You have to complete that report by the end of the day." "You have to send in your rebate coupon." "You must make an appointment." "You'd better be on time tomorrow." "You'd better get that delivery here." "You'd better be careful."" You must adjust to this new system." "You have to fill out these papers." "You have to wait in line over there." "You should have brought that with you." "You'd better think about that." "Get that done as soon as you can."

Remember, be careful when you use any phrase that dictates to people what they must do. No one likes to be commanded or ordered to do things. Even if you're a manager or owner of your own company who has the authority to tell people what to do, the language you choose can make a difference as to whether or not people will willingly follow your instructions. They may do what you say, but they may not produce quality work or worse, you may lose their respect.

Other phrases you'd be wise to avoid are those that weaken your position. Notice the subtle differences in the following examples:

Avoid: "We think ..." and "We believe ..." Instead, substitute "We are ..." or "We know ..."

- Poor: "We think you will be completely satisfied by the results of our marketing campaign."
- Better: "We know you'll be completely satisfied by the results of our marketing campaign."

- Poor: "We believe that the parts we provide will help you reduce your overall costs."
- Better: "We know the parts we provide will help you reduce your overall costs."

The words you use can make or break your ability to influence people. You may have the greatest ideas, the most logical proposals, the best products and services, but if you're unable to choose the right words to express your thoughts, it really won't make much difference.

Memorize Verbal Cushions

Of course, influencing people would be easy if all we had to do was present our ideas and wait for them to eagerly say, "Yes, I'll take two," or "You're hired. Can you start tomorrow?" Somewhere along the line, you're bound to face resistance. There are some techniques you can use to help influence people who challenge, object, complain, or question you. One that works well is the "verbal cushion." Those who excel in sales and customer service are skilled at using this technique. Verbal cushions are phrases that help soften the other person so that they don't perceive your words as threatening. If you Talk Smart and memorize these verbal cushions, you'll have them at your disposal when you face resistance. Here are some of the more common verbal cushions and examples of each.

"I understand your concern." / "I don't blame you for being concerned."

Let's say you've given a presentation to a potential client to secure a management-consulting contract. The client says, "I like your ideas, but frankly you've only been in business for six months. I'm not sure you have the experience to pull this off." You might reply, "I understand your concern. I'd be nervous, too, but three of our top consultants have worked in other consulting firms and bring over 15 years experience to the table."

"Others have asked me the same question."

You submitted a bid to be a subcontractor on a construction project. The general contractor says, "Your bid came in the lowest. In fact, it was so low, are you sure you'll be able complete the work without going over budget?"

You can reply, "Others have asked me the same question. We've completed twelve major projects in the past two years, and not once have we gone over budget. In fact, on five of those contracts, we came in under budget."

"I can surely appreciate why you'd feel that way."

You've introduced new audit procedures in the warehouse, and the employees are balking that it will take extra time to fill orders. You respond, "I can surely appreciate why you would feel that way. Our business is based on filling orders quickly, but Accounting has noticed that some of our merchandise has been misclassified and it's important that we keep more careful track of it."

"I'm sorry that happened to you. Let me take care of this immediately."

A customer complains that she's been waiting for over an hour to get her car serviced. You reply, "I'm sorry that happened to you. No one should have to wait for an hour. Let me take care of your car immediately."

"I am aware of that. I've thought it over, and I feel that ..."

You've just proposed to the owner of the company that the company should offer 24/7 service. The owner objects, saying that it would drive up personnel costs. You answer, "I'm aware of that.

I've thought it over, and I feel that within six months, the increased personnel costs will be offset by increased sales once potential customers can take full advantage of our increased service hours.

"I completely understand your situation."

You have asked an employee to come in on the weekend to finish a proposal by Monday. He hesitates, saying that he could really use the time off to recharge his batteries. You reply, "I completely understand your situation. I'm feeling like I'm getting ready to burnout myself. But tell you what, if you come in over the weekend, I'll give you Monday off as well as next Friday."

"I appreciate your sharing that, but I don't agree."

An employee complains that the new salary structure will make it more difficult to get a promotion. You respond, "I appreciate your sharing that, and I don't agree. Everyone will transition to the new salary structure and we're still committed to making sure we prepare people for the next level in the company."

"I hear your point of view, but here's another we might consider ..."

The company you work for manufactures ornamental candles sold exclusively in small gift shops. You would like to try to market your candles in larger retailers, but the owner of the company thinks the price of your candles will make them cost-prohibitive to people who shop in retail chains. You answer, "I hear your point of view, but here's another we might consider. Yes, the average shopper might pass on our candles, but the high volume of traffic through a retail chain means that we'll still see increased sales."

"Based on my experience, I've found that ..."

You're an architect who's designed a model home for a builder who remains skeptical about the ease of building your design. You tell him, "Based on my experience, I've found that contractors not only find my plans easy to work from, but that they enjoy the uniqueness of the design."

Feel ... Felt ... Found

One well-known and frequently taught verbal cushion is the three-step process. I "Feel, Felt, Found" technique. Your verbal cushion is presented in three stages:
1. "I understand how you feel."
2. "I've felt that way myself."
3. "What I've found is ...."

Here's an example of how it works. Let's say you want an employee to begin making telemarketing "cold calls" in addition to the traditional "warm leads." She resists, claiming that she doesn't know if she could effectively talk to complete strangers. You might reply, "I understand how you feel. It's not easy trying to build rapport with a complete stranger. I felt that way myself the first time I made a cold call. What I've found is that if you're persistent and sincere without being overbearing, people will eventually respond positively to you."

A variation of this technique is to use "we" instead of "I" because using the plural subject adds additional credibility in that the person doesn't feel the situation is unique to him or her:
1. "We understand how you feel."
2. "Others have felt that way."
3. "What we've found is ...."

In the next chapter, we'll see how the use of verbal cushions will help you when you must deal with difficult people and situations.

Cooperative Phrases

Part of Talking Smart is using cooperative phrases that help to deter any resistance you might encounter. They make the other person feel as if you and he are in this together. You can influence cooperation with phrases such as: "I would appreciate it if ...," "Can I rely on you to ...," "What do you say we ..." "What can I do to help you ...?" and "I'm confident you will ...."

Talking Smart—or the words you say—are only a part of your ability to communicate with others. How you say things—your tone and expression—also affect the message you communicate. I call this "Sounding Smart."

Sound Smart

Enthusiasm is infectious. Learn to speak with vitality, clarity and inflection in your voice. Sound as if you're happy to talk with someone. The inflection in your voice is important. If your inflection is inappropriate, you'll sound insincere. Be sure to keep your words positive and remember that the words you choose become your behaviors. Keep your behaviors positive, as your behaviors become your habits.

Don't Let Your BodyTalk "Do You In"

Your ability to influence others is affected by what you say and how you say it. A third area that affects your communication is the non-verbal messages you communicate—whether you're aware of them or not. Let's look at a few techniques you can use to improve your non-verbal communication skills.

- *Maintain eye contact.* This is the most powerful non-verbal communication technique. It portrays trust and credibility and makes people feel they have your undivided attention.

- *Nod your head when asking for agreement.* It's subtle, but by doing this, you send a subtle signal that impels others to agree with you.

- *Keep your palms open when asking for acceptance or buy-in.* Open palms suggest sincerity and congeniality.

- *Respond to what you see.* This skill is essential! You need to be aware of not only the body language you project but the body language of the person you're talking to as well. Some things to watch for include raised eyebrows, hand wringing, smirks, rolling eyes, crossed arms or a stiff jaw. Their words may be telling you one thing, but if you study a person's body language, they might be sending a different message. For instance, if potential customers tell you they are excited by your proposal, but they sit with their arms crossed and held tightly to their chest, that should send up a red flag.

Finally, as we saw in the chapter, "For Sales Professionals Only," you need to know when to talk versus when to listen, and know when to shift gears. I've seen sales reps sell, sell, and sell their product, but never stop to listen to the needs and expectations of the customer. Also, I've seen sales people rehash a point long after the customer has been convinced (or even unconvinced). If you learn to read a person's body language, the cues I mentioned earlier will let you know whether to continue communication or not.

Ask the Right Questions

Many times, people won't readily state their opposition to your ideas. They might not want to face confrontation or perhaps they haven't fully identified what they dislike about your points. Whatever the reason, you can identify others' needs or challenges by simply asking questions to learn what's on a person's mind.

Remember: Questions lead to answers. Answers lead to rapport and rapport leads to uncovering what the other person wants to know. As you ask your questions, stay focused on the other person. You can do this by being "you" conscious, as in:

"How do *you* feel about our plan?"

"What's *your* opinion?

"What are *your* thoughts?"

"Would this be all right with *you*?"

"What's the most important thing to *you* about what we've just discussed?"

"What can I do to help *you* with your job?"

"What would *you* like me to do?"

"What do *you* think about ...?"

Here are a few examples of "you" questions to help you learn someone's opinions or discover what's on their mind:

"John, you haven't said anything all during the meeting. I'd like your input. What are your thoughts on this?" (This is important when you're dealing with a passive person.)

"Martha, I'm sensing that you aren't yet convinced that we should be pursuing this course of action. Be straight with me. Are you comfortable with this?"

"That is certainly an obstacle we're likely to encounter, Mrs. Jones. Do you have any other concerns with this project?"

"I think I've gotten everyone's reaction to the shipping arrangements. Do you have any concerns we haven't covered?"

"I think this plan will take us where we want to be next year. Do you think we're on target here?"

"So those are the reasons in favor of switching suppliers. Joe, you look concerned. Are you with me on this?"

"These renderings can be drafted within two weeks; but first, what are your reactions to the blueprints?"

"That's what I think the implications mean for customer service. What's your opinion?"

"John, you look troubled by the new production schedule. What are your feelings?"

"Ma'am, we can have a replacement part out to you in 24 hours. Would this be agreeable to you?"

"So, we've outlined seven initiatives we need to take. What's the most important thing to you regarding what we've talked about?"

"I want to make sure that we meet the deadline. What do you suggest I can do to help?"

"Foreign competitors might eat away at our market share. What's your gut feeling telling you about the situation?"

Asking questions is beneficial because they can provide you with insights you might not otherwise get if you simply present your ideas and assume that the other person will accept them just because you do. Asking questions also gives you the opportunity to observe the other person's personality and body language. Most important, when you ask another person for their input, you show you have a genuine interest in them.

Listen and Respond

We addressed the importance of listening to customers. After you've asked a question, make sure you listen to what the other person has to say and respond to what they're *feeling* and not necessarily their words. I've observed several people who ask a customer a question, but never really listen to what the customer has to say. If that's how you respond, then you might as well not ask questions in the first place. Listening in order to influence requires far more than opening our ears, and asking a disingenuous question is mere lip service, as in:

> Customer service rep: "So, Mr. Collins, we can arrange delivery at 10:00 a.m. tomorrow morning. How does that sound?"
>
> Customer: "Actually, I'm not sure our warehouse will be ready to accept incoming shipments by then. We're usually—"
>
> Rep: "I know what you mean. Our drivers have the best on-time service in the industry."

Did the customer service rep really know what the customer meant? He was so adamant about making sure the customer knew his company's excellent service record that he ignored the customer's concern about warehouse capacity at that time in the morning.

When you ask questions, make sure you let the other person answer completely and don't interrupt. Instead, ask them to tell more. Also, make sure you stick to their subject, and if possible use *their* words to get your point across. Let's look at how the previous exchange might have gone with better listening and response skills:

> Customer service rep: "So, Mr. Collins, we can guarantee delivery by 10:00 the next morning. How does that sound?"
>
> Customer: "Actually, I'm not sure that our warehouse will be ready to accept incoming shipments by then. We're usually pretty hectic trying to ship our outgoing orders. Our warehouse is simply too small to accommodate too much traffic."
>
> Sales rep: "Yes, managing incoming and outgoing shipments can be challenging. Tell me, what time of day do you prefer to receive shipments?"
>
> Customer: "Actually, we usually get our shipments out by noon, so we like to have our deliveries begin at 1:00 p.m.
>
> Sales rep: "Yes, we stress promptness with all our drivers. That's why our customers tell us we have the best on-time service in the industry. And a 1:00 p.m. delivery time is certainly fine with us."

This time, the sales rep didn't interrupt the customer. He took the time to let the customer explain what the problem was, showed how they can meet the customer's requirements, and reflected the customer's words to make his point about their exceptional on-time service.

Again, don't forget to watch a person's body language. As you listen and respond, listen to not only their words, but also what they may be thinking and feeling.

Paraphrase

To be sure you've understood the content of the other person's message, paraphrase what they say. Remember to use your own words, or you may be perceived as a person who gives lip service. Paraphrasing not only clarifies and confirms your understanding but also shows your interest and attention. Some common phases for paraphrasing include: "Oh, so you feel that ...." "You're concerned that ...," and, "You want to be confident that ...."

Here's how you might use them:

Customer: "I don't know. If we give your company the account, we still need to use your competitor, ABC Company, to supply us with the products that you don't produce. I don't want ABC's service to suffer because the size of the account will be reduced."

You: "You're concerned that, if ABC doesn't generate a lot of income from your business, they'll view you as a lower priority for them."

Customer: "Exactly."

Paraphrasing will help to make sure that you understand the other person's concerns. Once you comprehend their issues, you'll be in a better position to address those concerns, and ultimately, influence the other person to your ideas.

As you respond to others, you need to be as empathetic as possible. When conveying empathy, use your own words to reflect what you think the person's feelings are. This helps to validate what the other person is trying to communicate. Some examples of empathetic statements include:

"I understand why this has been a challenge."

"I'm sorry, I didn't know you were having trouble."

"You must have been very discouraged when you lost that account."

Empathetic statements help validate the other person's feelings as well as develop rapport with others.

ASK for What You Want

This may seem obvious to you, but I've seen many sales professionals deliver a dynamic presentation and fail to ask for the sale. This is commonly known as presenting the "close." Closing the sale is not only important in selling situations, but every time you want to influence someone. Following are effective examples on how to *ask for what you want!*

"Can I rely on you to ...?"

"This is important to me. Will you call me and let me know by the end of the day?"

"Would you like to work with us on the project?"

"Will you commit to coming in on time tomorrow and every day afterwards?"

"We would like very much to handle this project for you."

"Would it be okay if we have our client manager give you a call to set up our first meeting?"

You'll notice that in several of these examples, the request came in the form of a question or was followed by one. Here's a tip you can take to the bank: Ask a question *immediately* after stating what you want. The key is to make sure you move from your request to your question in *one breath* with no pauses. Try it and you may find that almost every time the other person says yes also. Just be sure that you never sound pushy! Read through these examples:

"What I can do is place a trial order for one month. Does that sound all right with you?"

"What I might suggest is that you come to the manufacturing plant and have a look around. Would you like to set up a time?"

"Here's what I'd like to propose: We can continue our discussion on this tomorrow. Would that be convenient for you?"

"What I'd like to do is contact your field vice-president. Would you be comfortable with that?"

"Our architect can help you with that. Would you like me to call her right now and have her call you back?

"I'm going to have this to you by Saturday. Would that be all right with you?"

So remember, influence is all about action, and if you don't give the other person a specific action to take, then all you've done is present your viewpoint.

To summarize this chapter, I mentioned earlier that I would tell you how to influence your boss to give you a promotion. Following is a true story about Andrea Stevens, a woman who worked for my colleague Barry Eigen back when he was CEO of HealthCare Corporation. Andrea knew the right way to approach her boss and influence him to get the promotion she wanted.

Andrea was a young woman who'd worked for Barry's company for three years. One morning, she asked to see him about something she said was, "A matter of great importance to me, to you, and the company."

Barry was intrigued. What could it be, he wondered, that would be of great importance to her, the company and him? She had him hooked.

Barry had a full schedule that day, so he made an appointment to see her at the end of the day. Several times during that day, he found himself wondering what Andrea was going to tell him. She worked in his bookkeeping department and because she reported to a level of management well below his, he didn't have the opportunity to get to know her very well. He was curious. Who was this gutsy young woman and what did she have to tell him?

On schedule, she came into his office, shook his hand firmly, looked him in the eye and said with confidence, "I'm glad you could see me. I know you're busy and I'll come straight to the point."

Barry really appreciated her foresight. His days were filled with consultants, salespeople, customers and employees, most of whom had difficulty coming to the point and made an arduous practice of beating around the bush in hopes of strengthening and justifying whatever arguments they were making.

"I came to you because I want you to know I am ready for more work and more responsibility. I believe I have both the talent and the capacity for more." Then, she concluded with the clincher: "And I'm *ready* for a new and bigger challenge."

Andrea was confident, direct and definitely to the point. She emphasized the word "ready." She chose the right words, and what she *didn't* say was just as important as what she *did* say. She didn't say, "I want more money." Certainly she wanted more, but she was wise enough to know she wouldn't have to spell that out for the boss. It goes without saying.

The point here is that, without the words, Andrea did ask for more money, but she asked in the boss's language—in a way that emphasized she was willing to work for it. She said she was capable of assuming greater responsibility and willing to put in more time, energy, talent and effort to increase her value to him by contributing more to the company. What she said clearly in capital letters was: "I'm capable of doing more. I want to do more. So let me do more."

Barry understood this immediately. Andrea had said it differently than the majority of employees say it. She said, "I want an opportunity to *earn* more money," in a way that was not only refreshing but also extremely powerful.

The next day, Barry met with her supervisor and shared the essence of their brief conversation. He suggested Andrea be given an opportunity to take on some new tasks and that her responsibilities should be enlarged as soon as she proved capable of handling them. Finally, he asked to be informed of her progress so he could personally congratulate her along the way and make sure each addition to her workload was accompanied by a bump in salary.

Andrea went on to work for Barry for ten years in all. In that time, she grew to become a vice-president. Obviously, she had the talent and skills to advance in the company. But without the courage to bring herself to Barry's attention and ask for *what* she wanted in the *right* way, she may not have advanced at all.

Chapter 14

"Finding Beauty in the Beast"—
Dealing With Difficult People

"Be sincere and true to your word, serious and careful in your actions; and you'll get along even among barbarians. But if you're not sincere and trustworthy in your speech, frivolous and careless in your actions, how will you get along even among your own neighbors? When you stand, see these principles in front of you; in your carriage see them on the yoke. Then you may be sure to get along."
— Confucius

What does dealing with difficult people have to do with being able to compete and win? It's a fair question. From the start of my business career, I learned that if I wanted to be productive and maintain a positive state of mind, I needed to be capable of handling the difficult people and situations or I'd lose the positive energy I started with each day. I realized the importance of conserving my energy for important business activities such as closing deals, strategizing, improving operations, seeking new business, servicing customers and making decisions.

That brings me to those difficult people who throw a wrench into your good mood each day—the Slackers and difficult personalities we all encounter in the business world. They can make life a real challenge. You can't always avoid these difficult people and most of the time you can't change them so you must handle them effectively.

Difficult bosses, employees, customers and coworkers are much more than mere challenges. If you can't handle and cope with them, they can hurt your productivity, dampen your morale, drain your energy, cause stress and simply make your job miserable. In the workplace, most of us think difficult people just "go with the territory." If they do, you may need a road map to get you through the obstacles. What you can do is learn how to communicate with them in a confident, competent and non-combative way, resulting in improved relationships. Do that and you can focus your energy on the most important person—the customer.

What does it take to co-exist with difficult personalities? It takes self-confidence, staying calm and using the right techniques. Here's an example from a woman who works for one of my clients and needed my help with a difficult situation.

Terri is a mild-mannered CFO who had to confront a supervisor in the rough and tumble world of construction. (There's a natural personality conflict in the making.) Terri told me, "I'd looked over the construction expenditures for a project and noticed that the actuals far exceeded the projected. Material costs seemed to be in line, but labor was running too high. Now the construction supervisor for the project, Dave, didn't exactly have a reputation for being a 'people person.' In fact, I considered him to be downright hardheaded. Nonetheless, I needed to confront him about the project overruns. When I arrived at his office, I said, 'Hi, Dave. I need to talk to you about the Phoenix Towers project. You're running way over budget. It looks as if your people are working a little slower than they should be.' "

Right here, I could see that she was setting herself up for trouble, for apparently, Dave bristled, "Are you saying my guys are lazy?"

"No, not at all. I'm saying that based on the number of hours put into the project so far, we should be further along than we are."

Dave was getting annoyed and said, "The weather's been bad this winter and everyone's bummed out. I have a good crew and they're working their tails off, and I don't really appreciate your b_ _ _ _ ing to me. You're not out there every day, so you don't know what it's like. Let me do my job and the project will get done."

Terri began to feel defensive. "The budget is *my* job and you need to make sure your crew is working as effectively as possible. I'm the one that has to take the heat if we go over budget."

Dave got up. "Listen, my guys are good workers. If you think you can do my job, then by all means, we'll see you at Phoenix Towers tomorrow."

With that, he swore under his breath and stormed out of the room.

It takes all kinds of people to make up this diverse world in which we live. Some are easy-going, considerate, helpful and reasonable. Others are Slackers who can be labeled "difficult people." It seems to be their special mission in life to make the rest of our lives difficult—sometimes downright miserable. Think back to when you were a child. As a child, you were able to avoid bullies by walking a different way home from school or ducking behind a bush. Sure, you may have been one of the rare kids who stood up to the bully, but that often came at a great price—missing teeth, black eyes, or perhaps you were sent to the principal's office. But as an adult, you can't always walk down a different corridor or duck behind a cubicle. You must learn to deal with difficult people because most of the time you don't have a choice. They can be your customers, your boss, your teammates or worse—employees you can't fire.

It boils down to one thing—conflict. A person can be difficult for many reasons. Perhaps they care only about their own self-interest. They may be angry because their career is stagnating, their personal life is falling apart, or simply because they are a "hot-head" who got cut off in traffic on the way to work that morning. They may have grown up in an environment were they learned that they were always able to get what they wanted by nagging people. Maybe they are usually nice people who, like Dave, have been under a great deal of pressure. As we discussed in Section 1, whatever the reason may be, it's not your job to try to figure out the reasons why the person is difficult. Chances are you'll never know and you don't need to. Your concern is not why the person behaves the way they do—that takes too much energy—but how you can deal with their behavior.

Rather than seeing a situation with a difficult person as a personality clash, it may be more helpful to view it as a conflict. In the Phoenix Towers project, Terri knew that Dave had a less than pleasant personality. Instead of focusing on that, she should think about what Dave might want from the situation. He's under pressure from the owner, the subcontractors and the superintendent to get the project done on schedule. Maybe he doesn't have enough people on his crew, or maybe he's frustrated with the amount of paperwork he has to submit to Terri. Whatever his reason, it boils down to a conflict between what Terri is trying to accomplish and what Dave is trying to accomplish.

Learn the Process

When I work with a difficult person, I've had a lot of success effectively managing my relationship with that person by following a simple five-step conflict management process. It's one Terri said she wished she had as crib notes on her hand that day she clashed with Dave. Here's what I shared with her.

1. Determine Your End Result

Keep in mind what you're seeking to get out of your interaction with a difficult person, and you'll be less likely to get sidetracked by unrelated issues or allow yourself to get caught in a clash over personalities. Concerning Phoenix Towers, Terri needed to talk with Dave about the project overruns. But what did she want as an outcome? Her goal wasn't just to talk about the cost overruns, but to get him to push his people a little harder and smooth things over with him. She wanted Dave to make sure his crew was working as efficiently as possible. Ultimately, her goal was to get the project completed on time and on budget. She needed Dave's cooperation to get this accomplished.

2. Determine conflicting purposes

In conflict situations, you have your issues but you must remember that other people have their own. More than likely, Dave isn't intentionally undermining Terri's desire to control the costs in the budget. That's in his best interest. But there may be other factors in conflict with that desire. His primary concern is to do a quality job on the project but perhaps he feels his crew might not be as competent as he would like them to be. If Terri addresses these concerns, she has a better chance for a meeting of the minds.

3. Put Yourself in the Other Person's Position and Choose Your Words Carefully

When dealing with a difficult person, it's easy to become defensive or attack the other person as you try to determine their issues. Since you can't control his or her communication, you must start with your own. First, put yourself in the other person's position as you listen. Ask yourself, "What is this person really trying to tell me?" Dave mentioned that the weather was bad, but he also took offense that Terri might think his crew is lazy. Notice how he mentioned a few times that his crew was good. If Terri looked beyond the surface of the words, she may have discovered Dave's real issues. Terri also needed to avoid being critical herself. Once she became defensive and said, "The budget is my job and you need to make sure your crew is working as efficiently as possible," she lost whatever opportunity she may have had to get Dave to open up. The less judgmental you are and the more you listen to the other party, the greater the likelihood you'll find deeper issues troubling a difficult person. Later, we'll identify some techniques to help you avoid judgmental statements.

4. Seek a "Win-Win" Resolution.

Once you have surfaced the other person's agenda, you can find a "win-win" resolution that will meet your end result and resolve the other issues as well. If you cannot create a resolution that addresses the other person's concerns, then the difficult person will never buy into a solution where they see no benefit for them. Let's say Terri found out that Dave felt his crew needed better training. Obviously, removing people from the project to train them would not fulfill her objective of bringing in the project on time and on budget, but perhaps she could ask the owner to have one or two senior people from another crew assist Dave's crew for a few days while a few of his people receive the needed training. Then both parties would have a "win."

5. Get Comfortable on a *Verbal Cushion*

I've already said this but it's worth repeating: "You can't always avoid difficult people, and most of the time, you can't change them. What you *can* do is learn how to cope with them by communicating in a confident, competent and non-combative way." Whether it's a subordinate who's perpetually tardy, a peer who's jealous of your accomplishments, or an irate customer who calls to complain and demands to speak to your boss, you must be able to respond to them in an effective manner. When someone challenges you or becomes defensive, you need to diffuse the situation. You can do that by memorizing the verbal cushions. These are designed to "cushion" their challenging or objecting words and focuses on their issues in a non-threatening manner. They communicate a sense of concern and cooperation.

The sample phrases below will help cushion a challenging statement and make a nice companion to the five-step management process. If you memorize the verbal cushions identified in the previous chapter—"I can see why you would be upset," "I don't blame you for feeling this way," "We need to look at this more carefully," "I'm sorry, let's fix this," etc.— you'll get better results. Let's see how a few of these might work in some situations you might face.

You're discussing the new budget figures with your coworker:

   Larry: "I think you're way off on the supplies estimates. You need to rethink that. You really missed the boat on this one."

   You: "I can see why you might feel that way. However, the construction codes in Plainville are different. To meet the code, we'll have to order more expensive materials."

   Larry: "Oh, I forgot about Plainville's stricter codes. You're right."

Your sales manager is unhappy with the report you hurriedly put together to turn it in on time:

   Manager: "I have your sales report from last month. Didn't you even notice that your sales leads and sales closed don't reconcile?"

   You: "I'm sorry, Jean. Please give me a few minutes and I'll correct them. Last week was really hectic and I'd appreciate your understanding. I'll be sure it doesn't happen again."

You're meeting with a client to review the cost estimates to start a new Internet sales strategy:

   Client: "I don't believe these estimates. They're at least fifteen percent above what we discussed last week over the phone. You said you were confident you wouldn't exceed what I told you I'd lined up from the bank and the investors. Now I have to go back and tell them the cost estimates were wrong. They were reluctant to finance the project to begin with. Now what do you expect me to do?"

   You: "I can see why you would be upset."

   Client: "You're darned right I'm upset. Do you know how hard it was for me to get those investors?"

You: "I see where you're coming from. Let's stay on target with your needs. Let's review the estimates and I'll show you where and why the expenses are higher. When we're done, you'll see the more costly changes in my proposal will make your order fulfillment process more cost-effective and efficient. I'm confident that the enhancements I have recommended will prevent you from experiencing what many of your competitors have—costly and publicly embarrassing service delays. With a better service capability than your competitors, I believe you'll get higher sales than we first estimated. Using this logic I think your investors will be willing to put up the extra financing."

Client: "Okay, let's see what you've got."

Your overworked employee comes to you to vent a complaint:

Joe: "I can't work well with this team. They're simply not co-operating with each other and Lea and Chad aren't pulling their weight."

You: "I can see you're frustrated and I'm glad you came to me with this. Let's try to figure out how to get them to deliver for you."

An employee who is a chronic complainer gripes about a new order processing system:

Carol: "I think the new system stinks and so does everyone else. It's too hard to learn, and I don't see why we had to accept it just because that creepy consultant told you it would be more efficient."

You: "I understand how hard it can be to learn a new system. I've had to do it myself. Let's get someone to help you so we can make the transition a little smoother for you. Everyone needs to pull together to make this work because the system is here to stay. No one expects you to learn it overnight. Take it one day at a time and please don't be negative around the folks in your department who are doing their best to adapt to it, too. Can I rely on you for this?"

It will take practice using these phrases but, once you learn your lines, you'll agree that the use of these and other similar phrases that cushion a person's demeanor will work more often than not. Of course, it's not always easy to stay in control. When challenged, your first reaction might be to snap at people or become defensive and entrenched in your position. The beauty of verbal cushions is that they're still effective even if you're wrong. If you realize you're wrong, many of them can help calm down the other party so they can get past their feelings and on to resolving the situation. If you're correct in your position and the other party is too clouded by emotion to see it, using verbal cushions can help ease the transition from their being in a highly emotional state, to one where they may more clearly see your point of view.

Admit When You're Wrong

One of the most difficult people to deal with is the individual who is never wrong about anything. We've all encountered someone like that. Participants in my seminars tell me that type of person "irks" them more than anyone. When you know from the bottom of your toes that someone is wrong about something, don't waste your breath in efforts to change this person's point of view unless it's something really serious. On the other side of the coin, if *you* have made a mistake, handled a situation inappropriately, or misinformed someone, be sure to say, "I'm sorry. I was wrong." Or, "You're right. I stand corrected." This displays good character.

If Only It Were Always Rosy

Life is not always rosy. There are times when you simply need to confront someone and dish out criticism. This can be challenging to your communication skills—especially when dealing with Slackers or if any type of confrontation makes you uncomfortable. It amazes me how many people tell me they hate confrontation. And, how many managers tell me they don't have the time to use psychology on people—they just chew them out and be done with it. Is this a way to retain employees, promote goodwill and prevent turnover?

Most people have delicate egos, so you need to correct inappropriate behavior while, at the same time, protect the ego of the person involved. If you deliver criticism in a negative, harsh way—however right you are—you may permanently damage your relationship with the other person. You may get the behavior change you demand but the cost will come high: lack of trust, unmotivated employees and hostile coworkers. The following tips will help you communicate in a positive and non-threatening way when you need to dish out criticism.

1. Privacy Please

No one likes to be criticized in front of others. While this might seem too obvious and unnecessary to point out, you'd be surprised how often I'm appalled to hear about a manager or supervisor who has made critical comments to someone in a group setting. I think perhaps they were angry and lashed out the first chance they got. Perhaps it came up in the context of a team meeting. A participant in one of my seminars once told me how he received a "friendly" dressing-down by the group's director during a manager's meeting. A third party had inadvertently left some important personal recognition items out of a recent department meeting. Even though he was willing to take responsibility, the director chose to criticize him in front of his fellow managers. Everyone felt uncomfortable … except this director who was oblivious to her insensitivity. In the eyes of the other managers and mine, she was out of line.

When you need to deliver criticism, invite the person into your office when others will not notice, go to the cafeteria and discuss the problem over a cup of coffee, or speak to them before or after work. Just be sure you're discreet. You'll never win over anyone if you destroy someone's self-esteem in front of others—even if they have done wrong. In my opinion, berating someone in front of others is a mortal business sin and demonstrates a lack of class.

2. Preface Criticism with a Positive Statement

When you begin a conversation with a negative statement, you immediately invite the other person to put up their defenses. For instance, if you begin a conversation with, "Tom, the report you turned in yesterday was full of errors," Tom will feel defensive and make the rest of the conversation that much more difficult. Instead, try, "Tom, last week's report was very helpful in our discussion with the CEO and I'm glad to see that you turned in this week's report early. I was looking through it though, and noticed a couple of errors I'd like to point out."

One thing to keep in mind, however. Refrain from using "but" as the transition between your positive statement and the criticism. "But" is the other shoe that most of us immediately listen for, as in: "Thanks for giving me your input, *but* you don't understand the problem."

3. Don't Make Criticism Personal

Criticize what the person has done wrong—not the person. You don't want to focus on a personality trait. Since you're looking for a particular behavior change, focus the criticism there. Avoid saying, "Sally you're so insensitive. It really stunk when you laughed at our new service rep when he was trying to handle that irate customer." Instead say, "Sally, you know it's never appropriate to laugh at someone when they are working with a customer— especially someone who just started with the company. I don't think you intentionally meant to poke fun, but please don't do that again. We all need to be more supportive of each other. Can I rely on you for that?"

4. Supply a Positive Outcome

A person needs to see that, if an inappropriate behavior is corrected, something positive will result from it. Correcting inappropriate behavior should lead to future rewards. For instance, "Joe, if you go back and redo the Johnson analysis, I'm confident this client will be looking to you for future consultations." This will give Joe positive motivation to correct his mistakes.

5. Ask for Cooperation

Even if the person is a subordinate you should never *demand* that he or she change the behavior: "Beth, I'm tired of you coming in late all the time. From now on, you'd better be on time." You may be well within your authority to demand someone change a behavior but by doing so you'll create hostility. "Can I rely on you to …?" is a great phrase. It would be more effective to say, "Beth, we have a lot of work to get done in our unit and it's important to get here on time. You always do a good job for us once you're here. Can I rely on you to be here by eight?"

6. Only One Criticism to Each Offense

There may be multiple problems associated with a particular act but if you bring them all up at the same time, you're less likely to get the results you want. Be selective. Pick the most important behavior and work on that first. For instance, avoid, "Charlie, I was counting on you to get your part of the report to me yesterday. Now I won't be able to add my pieces by Friday. I don't think you were very interested in getting the report done on time and you never ask for help when you're in way over your head. I asked you to call me when you were almost through and you never did."

It would be more effective to focus on one of those issues, "Charlie, it was important to get your part of the report to me by yesterday. Now, I won't be able to add my findings by Friday. What prevented you from getting it done? (Then listen and offer help or suggestions, even if you'd like to slug him. Remember, you want to strive for win/win resolutions.) So next time you're not sure if you'll make it on time, please ask me for help."

7. Finish on a Good Note

When confronting someone to express criticism or address conflict, be sure you strive to maintain a positive working relationship. The person needs to know you can still be trusted and that any issues between you were not personal. "Rick, I'm glad we both understand the importance of double-checking figures. Let's be sure we do that from now on. Come on, let me buy you a cup of coffee and talk about who's going to win the Superbowl."

It's not easy to be able to criticize another's behavior with enough strength to elicit change and enough compassion to protect egos. Instructing people through criticism takes practice and patience. Consider the alternative: if you can't learn to do it effectively, you may find the label of "difficult person" applied to you.

A Final Word on Difficult People

Make it a personal challenge to tame the beast in people. I find it can even be fun—if you accept that difficult people are a part of life. Keep your sense of humor and use these skills to handle the difficult people you encounter. Don't allow them to get to you. Maintain a positive attitude and use positive self-talk ("I can handle this!") to help you deal with them.

Remember that personal growth occurs each time you properly handle the negative people and situations that confront you. It also occurs when you make it a habit to look for the good in every person—to find beauty in the beast.

Section 4

Keep Your Head in the Game

"God! I feel so burned out!"

I overheard this comment from a man who was speaking to his associate while standing in line to register for a conference. His friend's reply was, "I hear you. Hell, these days if you're not overworked, you don't have a job!" The first man nodded in agreement.

He's not alone in his belief. I mentioned earlier that years ago, before the computer revolution, I remember reading futurists' predictions about how much easier our lives would be once we entered the age of technology. Computers, they all claimed, would perform our menial tasks and provide us with more free time. I'm still waiting for my computer to transform my life from one of work to leisure. I won't hold my breath! As we all know, the truth is that computers enable work to be completed faster, and we're expected to do even more and to do it faster. And now that we have networks, modems, cell phones, pagers, and notebook computers, we've learned that there's no speed limit on the Information Superhighway.

Are you feeling as if you're living your life in the fast lane and just can't seem to find the exit-ramp? If you are, then you're like the many people I know who are caught up in the frantic pace of today's world. Many are living their lives speed-reading, quick-fixing, rush-houring, fast-tracking, and hustling and bustling themselves into a frazzle. Like them, you're so caught up in this frenetic lifestyle that you've become accustomed—no, *expect*—to be overworked.

Maybe you're an Overachiever who has programmed your brain to think that fatigue is next to godliness. For you, the phrase "hard work" has been transformed to "work too hard" and you never even noticed the change. You worry about work first thing in the morning, the last thing before you fall asleep, and probably wake up several times in the middle of the night wondering how you're going to get everything done the next day. Whatever happened to peaceful thoughts and feelings of calmness and inner peace?

I'm sure you can relate to the following: While speaking to a group of nurses, I asked them, "What's the biggest challenge you face on a daily basis?" One nurse immediately raised her hand and said with emotion, "I'm so busy taking care of the needs of my patients at the hospital and then going home to take care of the needs of my family. I'm always so busy taking care of *others*— when will I ever find time to take care of my *own* needs?"

Most people today are consumed by the responsibilities of their job and their responsibilities to others. There's always too much to do and too little time to do it. That's a given, no matter what you do for a living. "Where does the time go?" All our energy is taken away from us at work with appointments, paperwork, interruptions, putting out fires, meetings, projects, deadlines, voice-mail, e-mail, learning technology—the list is endless. Even our "free time" is taken up with personal chores. Not everyone can afford a full-time cook, live-in maid, nanny, laundry service and errand runner. This leaves us with little time for family, friends and leisure activities.

So what happens next?

Do you sometimes get a feeling in your gut that your life could be better? Do you feel you have "paid your dues" and want to see the rewards? Or perhaps you're searching for more meaning and purpose in your life.

I'm surprised at most people's lack of resourcefulness when it comes to creating balance in their lives—an important act which, when accomplished, ensures happiness in their lives. The business world in itself is a competition, and almost exclusively a head-game. In this final section, I share some valuable lessons I've learned that will help you handle the heat of the competition and create balance between your business and personal lives. If this section seems unnecessary to you, I'll remind you time and again that I've seen people fail to beat the competition simply because they were unable to handle the pressure. You may be beating the competition, but it will be a hollow victory if you self-destruct before the finish line. This final section provides some self-management strategies to help you compete more effectively.

Chapter 15

Avoid Job Burnout

The modern term "burnout" needs no explanation for today's busy business professionals. Too many people have told me they often live for days at a stretch when they experience stress, irritability, anxiety and inability to concentrate. These are all serious signals that burnout may be about to occur. Those who do manage to avoid burnout tell me it's a constant challenge to prevent it from happening to them. These are the realities of today's world.

Full-blown burnout can manifest itself in restlessness, depression, chronic fatigue, sleeping and eating disorders, anxiety attacks, blood pressure problems, heart disease and more. The wife of a client once confided in me that her husband—a vice-president of a prominent corporation—had been rushed to the hospital several times over the past few years with symptoms of a heart attack. Each time the diagnosis was an anxiety attack. I was shocked to learn this because whenever I'd seen him, he'd always appeared to be so easy-going.

I've experienced some of these problems myself, not during the start-up time of my company when business was a struggle but once I was experiencing great success. I've always had a lot of energy but, at that time, I was acting as if I were a machine and pushing myself too hard. I remember standing in line at a hotel reservation desk, exhausted after taking a "Red Eye," and I lost my temper when the clerk told me my room wasn't ready. "I specifically asked for early check-in and was assured my room would be ready. I'm the speaker for this big group!"

Now this was definitely not my style. Normally, I'd have said, "I'll just check my bags and relax by the pool until the room's ready. Won't you please do all you can to help me out?" But, I was irritable, running on empty and lost my cool. I worked myself into frenzy and had a headache the rest of the day. This was my wake-up call that burnout was imminent.

You can't "skip your turn" in the game of life so you need to maintain balance. So here are some proven self-management methods that will assist you in your efforts to avoid burn-out and stay secure and unwavering in the competitive sea in which you swim daily.

Stay Calm Under Pressure

As soon as you recognize you're becoming stressed, take a deep breath and remember that everyone has days and times like these when they are under pressure and feeling deluged with too much to do. Let's say you're getting ready to tackle a big project with a short deadline. You may feel as if you cannot possibly accomplish all that needs to be done. If panic sets in, don't worry. It's normal. Just feel the fear briefly, and then let it go. Envision the project as completed; it will give you the encouragement you need to get started. See the deliverable you've produced and the people you've impressed. Then roll up your sleeves and get going.

Most of us have numerous projects with deadlines. Here's a quick organizational skill that will help you stay in control of your work and help you remain calm under the pressure of many deadlines:

- The moment you become aware of any deadline, write it down in red pencil on your monthly calendar or enter it in your planner software.
- Identify the major tasks that will get you to your deadline, and then list the sub-tasks under your major tasks.
- Determine the number of days needed to complete each task. Then, count backwards from the deadline to figure the latest start date.
- Write down an appointment with yourself as a reminder to get started. This will help you stay calm and avoid the pressure of meeting that deadline.

Instead of agonizing over all the work you have to do, say to yourself, "I have a lot I'm going to get done." This is how you empower yourself to accomplish tasks. You'll find that breaking a project down into definable steps will help reduce your anxiety level because you'll know what you need to accomplish by when. Leaving a major project undefined will cause you undue stress because you'll constantly worry whether or not you have enough time to complete it. Also, recognize that with all your good intentions, interruptions will occur and it's highly likely that you'll have to shift priorities—we all do. We all have fires that must be extinguished so take care of what's urgent and adjust your attitude so that you learn to accept changing priorities.

Manage Your Anxiety

The pressure of a deadline can cause anxiety, but confronting a difficult person can create even more distress because of the immediacy of the situation. You don't always have time to prepare a response to the conflict let alone anticipate it. Of course, the techniques you learned in "Dealing with Difficult People" will help you manage the conflict, but you may still feel stress over the situation.

Before, during or after a confrontation with a difficult person, when you feel the pressure begin to mount, the key is to remain calm. Maintain your composure and use the old "I can handle this" positive self-talk. Think of Steven Covey's principle: "Seek first to understand, then be understood."

In their own mind, everyone thinks they are right. Remember what we said about dealing with difficult people and situations—it takes all kinds of people to make up this world, and all of them have different personalities and agendas. You must learn to deal with them by simply accepting that fact. Don't let them get the best of you because it's not personal, it's business.

When dealing with confrontation, conflict or other sensitive situations, keep problems in their proper perspective. Things are rarely as bad as they seem during the stress of the moment. Therefore, don't immediately react to the emotion, but step back and ask yourself, "What is it that's *really* upsetting the other person?" Sometimes, they may just need to vent. Avoid being critical and judgmental of others, and be sure that you're not overreacting yourself. Some people wear their hearts on their sleeves, are overly sensitive and take things too personally.

One of my clients is a highly successful and prosperous owner of an equipment finance company. One day over lunch, we discussed the pros and cons of entrepreneurship. "The positive side," he said, "is being your own boss and the sense of accomplishment you feel when business is thriving, profits are high, and your salespeople are happy with their commissions. These make entrepreneurship worthwhile. The negative side occurs when business hits a slump and you experience anxiety."

Although he has more than sufficient funds in his personal bank account to retire, he feels an obligation to keep the company going so that his partner and employees can stay gainfully employed. He also shared the anxiety he feels when he has to make a decision that if wrong, can affect the financial well being of the entire company. "It's not easy being responsible for the welfare of so many people." Then he said something that stuck in my head: "Success in business requires controlling your anxiety."

You might not own your own business, but you still have many sources of anxiety:

- Your boss is counting on you to land the account that will make or break the company's profit for the year.
- You're meeting next week with a key customer who has been unhappy with your company's service.
- You promised a customer to deliver a product at a certain price, but your costing was off.
- Two of your best team members just resigned, as you're ready to begin a critical project.
- Your company has developed a new product line and you're having difficulty understanding how the equipment operates.

Whatever your source of distress, it's important to control your anxiety if you're ever going to solve the problem that's holding you back. Here are some additional ways to help control anxiety.

Eliminate Unnecessary Worry

You may know people who tend to worry about every single possible thing that might go wrong. This may be a learned habit from childhood, but whatever its source, it's an enormous waste of time and a bad habit that can increase your chances of experiencing burnout. For example:

- You have a presentation to deliver. You've done your homework and have created a powerful presentation, but you lay awake the night before worrying about whether your associate will remember to bring the data projector or whether the customer will buy into your proposal.

- Your supervisor has informed you of a departmental downsizing in a few months. You've already survived the last two and worry that maybe your time will be up. You're 50 years old and worry that you're too old for the new fast-track companies. Who's going to hire you? Maybe you'll have to sell the new house you and your wife just bought. Maybe you'll have to cash in your investments and flip hamburgers for a living.

- Your flight has been delayed, and you worry yourself sick about whether your new client will find your tardiness irresponsible. If only that weatherman had predicted that snowstorm on the East Coast ...

- Your company has hired a new vice-president for your area and you're worried about the changes she may want to introduce. You don't know what she has in mind, but you're sure it's going to make your life more difficult.

Will worrying about these things have an impact on what will actually happen? Will it do you any good? Of course not. None of these things are within your control. It serves no purpose to dwell upon these events because nothing you can do will change the outcome of what will ultimately happen. You need to break the habit of worrying about what you *can't* influence and focus on the things that *are* within your control. Worrying about what's going to happen blocks you from functioning effectively each day and keeps you from performing at your best.

All you can do is focus on what you can control. By applying this logic, you can eliminate unnecessary worry and avoid burnout. Maybe everything you worry about will work out just fine, or maybe your worst fear coming to pass will work out for the best. Maybe this is going to be "as good as it gets." But just maybe, the future is going to be good and you will have an abundance of resources and wisdom to handle whatever comes your way.

Attitude AGAIN!

To avoid burnout, it always helps to adjust your attitude. The world can be falling apart around you at work but that doesn't mean you have to fall apart inside. Be happy to be alive! Here's another wake up call: It's okay to *feel good* when things are not so good. As I said in the chapter on "Positive Attitude," let go of disappointments, lost sales and lost promotions, and move forward with the momentum of positive attitude. You're responsible for your own happiness, so give yourself permission to be joyful. Life is a gift and is not meant to be a struggle for us. The Slackers have never figured that out.

Use Stress as a Benchmark

Achievers know that if they're not having fun, there's something wrong. They never automatically accept stress as part of doing business, but they use it as a benchmark. As soon as they begin to experience too much stress, they "slow down in order to speed up" and figure they must be going about things the wrong way. They wisely recognize it as a warning sign to pay more attention to the self-management issues we discussed above and make adjustments. That includes making sure their lives have balance.

Achieve and Maintain Life-balance

Another issue that relates to avoiding burnout is the constant struggle for people to somehow obtain a sense of balance between their job and personal life. For many people, it's like a tightrope act that can cause anxiety and lead to burnout.

Without balance between your business and personal life, there's just no way you can beat the competition or even survive in today's fast-paced world without buckling under the pressure. If you're leading a high-pressure lifestyle like most of us, you need to take time each day for self-renewal, joy, and serenity in your life in order to stay fresh and creative, and enjoy life. Just as healthy eating habits take into account your nutritional needs, so does a balanced life take into account all your needs—family, friends, work, play, private, and spiritual time.

Achieving balance requires clearly defining your values and shifting a few hours each week from one activity to another. Unfortunately, it's not that easy. It requires coming to terms with your values and priorities, deciding what's most important and deciding to make the tradeoffs they require. Then, you need the discipline to create a structure that defines how you spend your time. If you think of your life as a jigsaw puzzle, you may have these pieces squarely in place—going to the office early, staying late to catch up on paperwork and working weekends. If this is the case, then where are the missing pieces of your life—the time for yourself and your family—to complete that puzzle? Finishing the puzzle and keeping your life in balance takes self-discipline.

Having a clear understanding of your values should determine how you spend your time. Values help define who you are and tend to evolve as you get older and wiser. When you ask people what they value in life, they usually respond with: children, family, relationships, financial security, education, spirituality, health/physical fitness, travel and volunteerism. These are the things they hold dear, and the things they feel are most important in life. They also mention the activities they most enjoy—boating, golf, music, movies, cooking, etc.

Leslie Charles, author of *Why Is Everyone So Cranky?* and five other books, enjoys a thriving business as a professional speaker and author. When asked how to achieve life-balance in our demanding profession, she replied, "As an 'equestrian sport athlete,' I have a whole other life besides speaking, writing and being an active member of the National Speakers Association. I own a horse (her name is Ladiebug) and I ride her regularly. We compete in horse shows during the summer. Dressage is an Olympic sport, with classical traditions that date back to Xenophon. It demands concentrated mental and physical skills for both the rider and horse.

"I take lessons regularly and pursue my sport seriously. It's very 'Zen-ish' and beautiful when done correctly. Keeping my horse and myself in competitive shape not only enables me to maintain life-balance, but it also prevents me from becoming overworked with business concerns."

The key to achieving life-balance is to build free time into your schedule so that it becomes routine. To do this, you must respect and cherish your free time and make it a habit to block out time on your calendar for *you*. Schedule activities that will regenerate your mind and your body. Here's how: Get your appointment book and look at your monthly calendar. Now, look at the next two weeks ahead. Take a pencil and make an appointment with yourself in the days ahead to do the things that nourish your mind and soul, and nurture relationships with those you love.

My theory is this: So much of our time is taken up with responsibilities that we need to "steal" a little back for ourselves. Block out a couple of evenings to see a friend or a family member. Block out days for bicycling, shopping, museums, family, movies, visiting, golfing—whatever you enjoy. If you don't have entire days, then block out a couple of hours—whatever you can afford. Here are more ideas that may be helpful to you.

• **Tune Out the Business World**

During this leisure time, recharge your batteries by blocking out all thoughts about business. This will enable you to generate creative ideas for, as you're engaged in leisure activities, your subconscious mind is contemplating decisions to be made and ideas to bring into your conscious mind. This will occur after you have rested.

Do this at a certain time each evening, as well. I have made it a personal *rule* that I never think about business after 8:00 p.m. unless I'm writing or attending a business function. I've practiced this habit for years and it's helped me to relax before bedtime.

• **Be Spontaneous**

Embrace spontaneity in your life. Do what you feel like doing when you want to do it. Accept last minute invitations and take short spur-of-the-moment trips when possible. Living your life planned to the split-second allows no room for spontaneity. I try to block out at least one day each month where I make absolutely no plans or commitments with anyone. Try it sometime. It will give you an opportunity to be spontaneous and provide some space where you can stretch, breathe and take life at a less harried pace.

- **Be Outrageous**

Here's a great way to regenerate your mind and body, especially if you feel you're about to experience burnout. Shift gears to charge your mental batteries by doing something you've never done before, even if it seems outrageous. When I started my company, I was feeling overwhelmed with all I had to learn and do. One day a friend said, "Let's go skating! Tuesday is adult night." I couldn't imagine two grown women skating at a roller rink but she persuaded me to go. The upbeat music was energizing and we had so much fun laughing at ourselves that it was definitely a stress-buster. You may not wish to put skates on, but doing these types of things will definitely reduce your stress level and keep your outlook fresh.

- **Who Says You Can't Do It? Break the Rules!**

Breaking your own rules helps prevent burnout and may be a luxury in which you forget to indulge. Who says you can't stay in bed late on Sunday and not get dressed or shaved? Who says you can't take a walk through the park with a friend at lunch hour? Who says that, on the spur of the moment, you can't go out after work to go to dinner or see a movie? Who says you can't let the housework go for a couple of days? Who says you can't block out an evening or a few hours on a weekend to do absolutely nothing? Who says you can't take a day off to take the kids to the beach? Who says you can't let clutter accumulate when you're working long hours?

Who says you don't "deserve a break today" and can't order out instead of cook? Who says you can't get up and dance even if you have no rhythm? Who says you can't have a picnic in the middle of winter? Who says you must be a "careoholic" and be overly responsible for the people in your life? Who says that doing the laundry is more important than getting on the floor with your child and listening to what she has to say about her day or playing a game with her? Who says you can't make time to listen to a friend in need? Who says you can't reverse daytime and nighttime activities to give a special flavor to your day off?

- **Just Say No!**

As Steven Covey tells us in *The 7 Habits of Highly Effective People*, "Learn to say no to activities that are not congruent with

your core values." For example, "I'd like to say yes, but it's important to me to spend time with my family tonight." Or, "I'm sorry, I
really need to recharge my batteries this weekend." Or, "I'm sorry,
I've committed to coaching Little League this summer."

Easier Said Than Done?

As you've been reading, perhaps you've been thinking, "Oh,
sure, easier said than done." Why is it so hard for us to slow down
and relax? Earlier, I mentioned my childhood neighbor who is now
a high-powered executive of an internationally prominent corporation with over 28,000 people who ultimately report up to him. He
has more responsibility than anyone I've ever known—both personally and professionally. Not only is he constantly receiving calls
from their branches throughout the world, but also he and his wife
are parents of four children.

One day, I asked him, "With all the long hours, international
travel, public speaking, client meetings and writing, how do you
keep your life in balance?" He gave me many ideas, but what remained in my mind was what he told me about how he maintained
balance when his children were small. He said, "I took my family
to our home in the country almost every weekend and would invite
a client and their family, as well. This way, both of us could squeeze
in business discussions *and* spend time with our families. I also
took my children to the country club and permitted them to take
turns driving the golf cart while I played. Other than when I was
concentrating on hitting the ball, I was completely focused on listening to them share stories of what happened at school that week."

A balanced life creates harmony between your business life and
your personal life. Don't leave the activities of life-balance at the
bottom of your "to-do" list. When you incorporate leisure into your
life, you'll be able to handle the grit and grind of working in today's
real world. Alternate hard work with hard play. Balance giving with
receiving, and taking care of your responsibilities to others with
taking care of yourself. When you do, you'll be smarter and more
creative than your competitors because you'll be enjoying your life.

Chapter 16

Create Meaning and Purpose in Your Life

In this book, I've shared a great deal of what I have learned about the business world. I hope you've found great value in reading it. Indeed, I'm *honored* that you've read it. As I write this final chapter, I realize how many thousands of business books are published around the world each year and that if I didn't include these final messages from my heart, I'd have regrets. While on the competitive treadmill, you can enrich your life and find greater meaning and purpose in it by remembering the following messages.

Life is For Doing, Learning, Helping and Enjoying

The Achievers of this world have learned to love their work. Keep your heart open to all the experiences your job can teach you about yourself and the business world. Have enthusiasm for your work and your life. If you make this apparent to others, it will spread to your customers, coworkers and those you love.

Develop yourself in new ways by learning new skills and setting your sights toward higher goals and personal growth. Maintain an upbeat attitude and accept that life isn't always fair, that problems will occur and that you're likely to make a few more mistakes along the way. Take obstacles in stride, keep a proper perspective and maintain your sense of humor. Remember that, each time you laugh, you inject a surge of positive energy into your body.

Forget About the Past, But Appreciate It

Don't let the past hold you back from winning. It's easy to hang on to past mistakes, and career or life's disappointments. It's far better to look upon them as learning experiences and appreciate them for what they've taught you. The past is finished. Whatever you have or have not achieved, you can't change it. Learn from it, forgive yourself if you must, forget about it and focus on what you *can* impact—today and the rest of your life. Do some mental housecleaning. When you find yourself fretting over disappointments of the past, stop wasting your energy and seek new challenges, peace and contentment for your life. Then, you'll be able to advance to higher levels of success and begin to live your life to its fullest potential.

Clean Out Your Closets

It's obvious how strongly I feel about the role positive energy plays for those who seek success and prosperity. When I started my speaking business, I realized people who did not share the same values were draining much of my energy. I also observed that the most successful people around me had no tolerance for negative people, for Achievers know that these individuals can be toxic to their well being.

If you realize that you're spending your valuable time and energy with others who do not share the same values or have interests which have grown apart from yours, I encourage you to eliminate or at least lessen the amount of time you spend with them, because they're probably not adding any real value to your life. Perhaps you've known some of these energy-zappers for a long time and have simply outgrown them. I'm not suggesting you need to be hurtful to others, but it isn't fair to a hard-working person to invest time in relationships that bring no enjoyment.

Discover "Who You Are" and "Who You Want to Be"

Mark Twain said, "Keep away from people who try to belittle your ambitions. Small people always do that, but the really great make you feel that you, too, can become great." Initiate relationships and spend time with people who not only encourage you, but also provide real friendship. Surround yourself with loyal friends who genuinely care about you. Be sure you have at least one close friend on whom you can count to give you a kick in the pants when you need it. Associate with brilliant Achievers who have meaning and purpose in their lives and are dedicating themselves to worthy attainments that make a vital difference for their family, friends, neighbors, coworkers and customers, as well as themselves.

View Change as Excitement

Look upon our changing world as an exciting time to be alive. Yes, there's competition all around us, but it's always been there. And as more sophisticated technology emerges and our world changes with it, consider this: "Technology Changes, Psychology Does Not." Amidst all the changes occurring around us, what things have changed that are truly important to *you*? None! Family, friends, health, peace of mind, stability and comfort are still the things that are important to you.

Create Meaning and Purpose

I recall hearing: "the purpose of life is to have a life of purpose." How true. We each have a life to live, one that has meaning and direction. I know a lot of people who take themselves and their work too seriously. Of course, our work and our success are important, but in the end, it shouldn't be what defines you. Understanding this took me a long time for, as a young woman, I defined myself as a person by my professional achievements. Over the years, I began to realize that, most likely, no one at my funeral would say, "She was such a successful businesswoman!" I hope they'll remember me for my upbeat spirit, my willingness to take risks and my commitment to my family and friends.

Value Time and Friendship

Respect time and don't waste it. Recognize that time is our most precious commodity and that it's surely more important than money. Gayle Olson, my closest friend, was a vibrant woman who had an incredible zest for life. She had the best of everything—loving husband, wonderful family, beautiful home, adoring friends, good looks and a successful career as a radiology technician. Then lung cancer stole it all away from her much too early. Losing her was devastating to me, as it was she who always encouraged me in my every endeavor and gave me that kick in the rear when I needed one. The loss of this dear friend was my wake-up call on the importance of time and the value of loyal friendship. I know now how valuable our time is here on this beautiful blue planet Earth, and how important it is to make time for the people who are important in my life.

If, on the last day of your life, someone offered you time or money, you undoubtedly would ask for time. Joan Baez said, "Tomorrow is not promised to any of us. We can't choose how or when we're going to die, but we *can* choose how we're going to live. Live now!"

Achievers help themselves, and help others and make a difference in their lives. When you commit to becoming a positive person who's making a positive difference in the world, and in the lives of those you touch in your business and your personal life, then you'll be an Achiever. You'll also be in a powerful position to compete and win in today's real world.

> "We make a living by what we get,
> But we make a life by what we GIVE."
> — Winston Churchill, 1950

> **"Your MIND is a human instrument of the finest order,**
> **And the most delicate balance.**
> **Tune it as if it were a fine violin**
> **To achieve success in all your endeavors.**
> **Play it with passion, rhythm and great expression.**
> **Then, you will live your life in harmony with others,**
> **And to its fullest potential with yourself."**
> — Christine Corelli, 2000

About the Author

Christine Corelli is an international speaker, author and entrepreneur who is dedicated to helping organizations and their people to lead, compete and win in a changing world. Her seminar topics include: sales excellence, creating high performance through change, establishing customer loyalty, and communicating to influence.

Christine has been invited to speak to prominent corporations and associations that include clients such as Panasonic, Sears, Reynolds Aluminum, Nissan, United Van Lines, DaimlerChrysler, Northern Trust Bank, Exxon, K-Mart, the American Society of Association Executives and the American Economic Development Council.

She has crafted a unique and compelling presentation style. Her clients can attest to how she delivers with great enthusiasm and attention to detail. For further information on her programs,* to learn about other educational products she offers, or to share how some of the strategies in this book have worked for you, contact her office at (800) 611-9968.

Or, visit her Web site at: www.christinespeaks.com

* Christine's Most Requested Programs are:

• Wake Up and Smell the Competition
Sales Excellence/Business Growth/Maintaining a Competitive Edge

• The Top Banana is Supported by the Rest of the Bunch
How to Create a High Performance Workplace Through the Midst of Change; Managing Change/ Employee Motivation/Employee Retention

• The Customer of the Future—Will Tomorrow's Customers Be Yours?
Service Excellence/Establishing Customer Loyalty/Consumer Trends

• The Art of Influencing People
Communication Skills for Managers, Sales Professionals, and Business Leaders

Products by Cardinal Business Press

Additional copies of *Wake Up and Smell the Competition: They're Closer Than You Think*
— $19.95 plus $4.00 S & H (Total: $23.95 / $26.95 to Canada)

Selling Savvy for the New Millennium (90 min. audio cassette tape)
— $19.95 plus $4.00 S & H (Total: $23.95 / $26.95 to Canada)

Maximizing Personal Effectiveness (90 min. audio cassette tape)
— $19.95 plus $4.00 S & H (Total: $23.95 / $26.95 to Canada)

For credit card orders (Visa, Mastercard and Discover), please call toll-free:

1-888-281-5170

If paying by Money Order, please mail to:

QP Distribution
PO Box 220
Goleta, CA 93116

If paying by check, please mail to:

Cardinal Business Press
6401 Lincoln Avenue, Suite 204
Morton Grove, IL 60053

Recommended Reading

Bucaro, Frank. *Taking the High Road*. Elgin, IL: FCB & Associates, 1999.

Byham, William C., Ph.D., with Jeff Cox. *Zapp! The Lighting of Empowerment*. New York: Fawcett Columbine, 1988.

Collins, Eliza G. C., and Mary Anne Devanna. *The New Portable MBA*. New York: John Wiley & Sons, Inc., 1998.

Covey, Stephen. *The 7 Habits of Highly Effective People*. New York: Simon and Schuster, Inc., 1989.

Eigen, Barry. *How to Think Like a Boss and Get Ahead at Work*. New York: Carol Publishing Group, 1999

Geist, Sam. *Would You Work for You?* Toronto, ON: Addington and Wentworth, 2000.

—— *Why should Somebody do Business with You Rather than Someone Else?* Toronto,ON: Addington and Wentworth, 1997.

Gitomer, Jeffrey. *Customer Satisfaction is Worthless, Customer Loyalty is Priceless*. Austin, TX: Bard Press, 1998.

Glanz, Barbara. *Care Packages for the Workplace*. New York: McGraw-Hill, 1996.

Herman, Roger, & Gioia , Joyce *How to Become an Employer of Choicer*. Greensboro, NC: Oakhill Press, 2000.

Kragen, Ken. *Life is a Contact Sport: Ten Great CareerStrategies that Work*. New York: William Morrow and Company, Inc., 1994.

Mandino, OG. *University of Success*. New York: Bantam Books, 1982.

Mcormack, Mark H. *What They Don't Teach You at Harvard Business School: Notes from a Street Smart Executive*. New York: Bantam Books, 1984.

Meisenheimer, Jim. *50 More Ways to Sell Smarter*. Libertyville, IL: Helbern, 1996.

Morrison, Ian. *The Second Curve: Managing the Velocity of Change*. New York: Ballantine Books, 1996.

Nelson, Bob. *1001 Ways to Reward Employees*. New York: Workman Publishing Company, Inc., 1994.

Ray, Michael and Rochelle Myers. *Creativity in Business*. New York: Doubleday, 1986.

Index

Memo

Date: 5/1/2003

To: Universal Electric Products Co., Inc.
Automation Sales People and Management Staff

Subject: Wake up and smell the Competition, They are closer than you think!
Written by Christine Corelli

"Any time customers have contact with someone in your company for any reason, they are evaluating your company and whether or not they will continue to do business with you." What kinds of answers do customers get when they contact your billing department? What does the shipping department do when a customer has a special request? How do your service technicians treat people when they go to the customer's office? All this contact comes under the heading of marketing your company, winning the customer's confidence, or sending the customer somewhere else!.

You know it. Do all of your employees know it? Customers are really turned off when a worker is willing to do only what is convenient for him rather than what is good for the customer. How much business are you losing because of this? Do you hear what your people are saying over the phone and on the project site? This book is full of "real world" ideas and solutions to problems plaguing today's businesses and business professionals.

Universal Electric Products Co., Inc. has purchased the attached booke to help our sales team reach new levels of achievemnt. We want everyone to read this book prior to our June Sales Meeting (Date still to be determined..aim for 2nd week). As a salesperson, in order to grow, you must be able to accept criticisim and critic yourself.

In Chapter 1, it states that there are three types of people. Which type are you? Everyone must give a brief description of what type they are at the sales meeting, put it in writing and be ready to discuss why you are what type or types. This is to help you grow and more importantly to help Universal Electric Products Co., Inc. grow as a company in this current economy.

Another assignment may be given out, so please be prepared. Please read this and be ready to discuss it at the June sales meeting.